立春

ひのもとのはるのしるしに
しもみえぬ風こそそらに
ふきそめにけれ

山霞

こきちりてみねの
あらしもよそに
ちるこすゑのみどりを
とほく

湖邊霞

めぐみれ人のこゑにや
しらゆきのみねのよの山を
よそにみるらむ

嶋

まがきもりうすかすみへる
みちはしらぬをきなみの
なはしらすやへのしま
もろこしまでもみゆらむ

The Eight Female Emperors of Japan

A Brief Introduction
to
Their Lives and Legacies

Kiyoko Takagi

Translated by
Masako Hamada, et al.

《Emperor Suiko》

Oharida Palace site (estimated location)
Asuka Village, Nara Prefecture.
(Image provided by Shinjinbutsu Orai-sha.)

《Emperor Kōgyoku and Emperor Saimei》

Asuka Itabuki Palace site (estimated location)
The site where Soga no Iruka was defeated by
Prince Naka no Ooe and Nakatomi no Kamatari.
Asuka Village
(Image provided by Shinjinbutsu Orai-sha.)

《Emperor Jitō》

Site of the Imperial Council Hall (*daigokuden*) of Fujiwara Palace.
Fujiwara was the first fully-developed capital in Japan. It was there that the three emperors,
Jitō, Monmu, and Genmei resided and attended to the state affairs for their three consecutive
regimes. (Emperor Genmei, however, moved to Heijō Palace when it was completed.)
Kashihara City (Image provided by Shinjinbutsu Orai-sha.)

《Emperor Genmei》

Site of Imperial Council Hall (*daigokuden*) of Heijō Palace. The Heijō capital was
constructed following the model of Chang'an, the Tang capital.
Heijō was the capital for approximately seventy years,
spanning the reigns of seven emperors from Genmei to Kōnin.
Sakichō, Nara City. (Image provided by Shinjinbutsu Orai-sha).

《Emperor Kōken》

Wooden plaque by Emperor Kōken

This plaque, made of Japanese cypress, bears the four Chinese characters, "Tō," "shō," "dai," and "ji" in Emperor Kōken's handwriting. Her penmanship reflects her strong personality. Owned by Tōshōdaiji Temple. (Image provided by Asuka-en.)

《Emperor Meishō》

Zuigu darani

It is said that when her mother, Tōfukumon-in, passed away, Emperor Meishō transcribed the Darani-kyō and prayed for the repose of her mother's soul.
(Owned by Jūzenji Temple. Image provided by Kasumi kaikan.)

"Jūzenji" plaque inscription

Emperor Meishō's calligraphy at the age of sixty-seven.
Her writing style was bold and vigorous.
(Owned by Jūzenji Temple. Image provided by Kasumi kaikan.)

The Eight Female Emperors of Japan

A Brief Introduction
to
Their Lives and Legacies

Kiyoko Takagi

Translated by
Masako Hamada, et al.

Fuzambo International

©2018 Fuzambo International Ltd.
All rights reserved.
Printed in Japan,

Hachinin no jotei by Kiyoko Takagi
©2002 Kiyoko Takagi

The Eight Female Emperors of Japan:
A Brief Introduction to Their Lives and Legacies by Kiyoko Takagi
©2018 Fuzambo International Ltd.; translated by Masako Hamada, et al.
First edition, 2018.

ISBN978-4-86600-052-7

2018 Fuzambo International Ltd.
1-3 Kanda Jimbocho,Chiyoda-ku,
Tokyou,101-0051,Japan
TEL +81-3-291-2578, FAX +81-3-219-4866
URL www.fuzambo-intl.com

Printing: Fuzambo International Ltd.
Bookbinding: Kato Seihon Ltd.

*In memory of Kiyoko Takagi,
a beloved colleague and friend.*

having come to where
the road of cherry blossoms
ends, I turn to look back —
the wind rises, and like a flood
the flower petals flow

sakura michi / hatsuru made kite / furimukeba /
kaze kite bōda to / hanabira nagaru

— Kiyoko Takagi

Table of Contents

Abbreviations	5
Select List of Premodern Emperors and Their Reigns	6
About the Author	9
Preface	11
Translators' Note and Acknowledgements	16
Introduction	19
1. Emperor Suiko	35
2. Emperor Kōgyoku	57
3. Emperor Saimei	74
4. Emperor Jitō	96
5. Emperor Genmei	137
6. Emperor Genshō	161
7. Emperor Kōken	182
8. Emperor Shōtoku	207
9. Emperor Meishō	226
10. Emperor Go-Sakuramachi	245
Conclusion	258
Contributors	261
Bibliography	264

Abbreviations of Texts

Go-Sakuramachi tennō gyosei	GSTG
Kokinwakashū	KKS
Man'yōshū	MYS
Nihon shoki	NS
Shoku Nihongi	SNG

Select List of Premodern Emperors and Their Reigns
(*female emperors in bold*)

Asuka period (538-710)

29.	Emperor Kinmei	539-571
30.	Emperor Bidatsu	572-585
31.	Emperor Yōmei	585-587
32.	Emperor Sushun	587-592
33.	**Emperor Suiko**	**592-628**
34.	Emperor Jomei	629-641
35.	**Emperor Kōgyoku**	**642-645**
36.	Emperor Kōtoku	645-654
37.	**Emperor Saimei**	**655-661**
38.	Emperor Tenji	661-672
39.	Emperor Kōbun	672
40.	Emperor Tenmu	672-686
41.	**Emperor Jitō**	**686-697**
42.	Emperor Monmu	697-707
43.	Empress Genmei	707-715

Nara period (710-794)

43.	**Emperor Genmei**	**707-715**
44.	**Emperor Genshō**	**715-724**
45.	Emperor Shōmu	724-749
46.	**Emperor Kōken**	**749-758**
47.	Emperor Junnin	758-764
48.	**Emperor Shōtoku**	**764-770**
49.	Emperor Kōnin	770-781
50.	Emperor Kanmu	781-806

Tokugawa (Edo) period (1603-1868)

107.	Emperor Go-Yōzei	1586-1611
108.	Emperor Go-Mizuno'o	1611-1629
109.	**Emperor Meishō**	**1629-1643**
110.	Emperor Go-Kōmyō	1643-1654
111.	Emperor Go-Sai	1655-1663
112.	Emperor Reigen	1663-1687
113.	Emperor Higashiyama	1687-1709
114.	Emperor Nakamikado	1709-1735
115.	Emperor Sakuramachi	1735-1747
116.	Emperor Momozono	1747-1762
117.	**Emperor Go-Sakuramachi**	**1762-1771**
118.	Emperor Go-Momozono	1771-1779
119.	Emperor Kōkaku	1780-1817
120.	Emperor Ninkō	1817-1846
121.	Emperor Kōmei	1846-1867

About the Author

Kiyoko Takagi
(1918 - 2011)

Dr. Takagi graduated from a program in Japanese Language affiliated with the Tokyo Women's Higher Normal School (now called Ochanomizu University Senior High School) in 1939. After World War II, she was a research student at the University of Tokyo and majored in Philosophy at Ochanomizu University. She then became a doctoral student in Religion at the University of Tokyo (1954-1960) and studied for a time at Harvard University. She was a Professor and Associate Director at the Inter-University Center for Japanese Language Studies (1961-1981). A visiting scholar at the Department of East Asian Languages and Cultures of Columbia University (1968-1969), later returned to Japan and became a professor at Ochanomizu University (1981-1984) and Toyo University (1985-1989). She received her PhD from Tokyo University in 1991.

Her book publications include: *William James' Religious Thoughts* (1971); *Life and Death in Literature* (1983); *Saigyō's Religious World* (1989), *Cherry Blossom: Its Holiness and Vulgarity* (1996); *Saigyō — I had given up all my attachments to this world* (2001); and *Hachinin no jotei* (2002). Dr. Takagi also published several collections of *tanka* poetry, including *The Light of Blossoms* (*Hana akari*) (1978); *Selected Cherry Blossoms* (*Ōkashō*) (1984); *Cherry Blossoms Once Again* (*Sakura futatabi*) (1990); *Evening Cherry Blossoms* (*Yūzakura*) (1998); and *Drops from Blossoms* (*Hana no shizuku*) (2006).

Preface

Memories of Dr. Kiyoko Takagi

Kimiko Murofushi, PhD
President of Ochanomizu University

It is a great honor to write the preface for the English version of *The Eight Female Emperors of Japan* by Dr. Kiyoko Takagi. I am grateful to Ms. Kikuko Sakamoto, president of Fuzambo International, for granting me this opportunity.

I first met Dr. Takagi as a student in her class while a freshman at Ochanomizu University. I took a six-month "Introduction to the Study of Religion" course, in which she lectured. I can vividly recall Dr. Takagi at the podium; her lectures were clear and direct. After the class I often asked her various questions, and she was always very generous in answering all of my questions thoughtfully and thoroughly. As a science major, my focus eventually turned to the relevant coursework, and so, after the class concluded, our paths would not cross again on campus. However, I always remember her class fondly, particularly Dr. Takagi's positive response to the report I submitted.

Twenty years later, I would never have expected her family and mine to be related. One of the senior board members of the Ochanomizu University Senior High School Alumni Association was Dr. Takagi's niece, whose daughter my nephew later married. And now I am writing this introduction for her work. A true pleasure!

First published in 2002 and reprinted in 2005, *The Eight Female Emperors of Japan* describes how these female emperors rose to the throne and details their lives and governance as recorded in such historical literature as *Nihon Shoki, Shoku Nihongi* and *Man'yōshū*. This is an academic book, but it is straightforward enough for younger readers in junior high school and high school to understand it.

The roles and achievements of female emperors in Japan's history have received little attention. There were eight female emperors in ten regimes. The first was Suiko (592-628) in the Asuka period (538-710), who was in the imperial position for thirty-five years, and the last was Go-Sakuramachi (1762-1771), who was the tenth emperor in the Edo period (1603-1868). This book clearly demonstrates how vital their ascensions were to the continuity of the imperial line. However, these female emperors were not merely intermediary agents; as readers will come to appreciate, they also had significant accomplishments in the political and diplomatic arenas during their reigns.

Preface   *13*

Congratulations on the publication of this English edition. I sincerely hope this book will be read by many readers throughout the world.

Kikuko Sakamoto
President of Fuzambo International

On mourning the loss of our beloved chancellor:

dear cherry trees
in the fields of Fukakusa,
I wish you would
have mercy and bloom
just for this year in black

fukakusa no/ nobe no sakurashi / kokoro araba /
kotoshi bakari wa / sumizome ni sake
[KKS XVI: 832]

I attended lectures about Japanese Literature and Religion through *Sakurakai* for a long time from Dr. Takagi, who was a scholar of historical Japanese poetry.

not a day goes by
without enjoying myself
reading aloud
the old poems, and transcribing
The Tale of Genji

ichinichi mo / kakuru koto naku / tsuzuke ori /
koka no ondoku / Genji no hissha

[Kiyoko Takagi]

I adore Dr. Takagi, who learned all of the poems in the *Man'yōshū*, *Kokinwakashū*, and *Shin-kokinwakashū* by heart. I was invited to join her poem writing group for the group's poetry journal, *Uchūfū*. The classroom was always full of students. Through her lectures, Dr. Takagi created an atmosphere of intellectual excitement. Dr. Takagi occasionally talked about cherry blossoms, and memories of the very precious time we spent in her lectures, as well as her sense of style in clothes, are precious treasures for us.

bathed in the dazzling
setting sun, cherry blossoms
glitter in gold,
in the dusk they shimmer in silver
in the pale light of lamps

irihi abi / sakura wa kin ni / kageyakite /
tomoshibi no moto ni / gin ni shizumoru

[Kiyoko Takagi]

I cherish Dr. Takagi's poems, which reflect her deep
insight and sharp intuition. I appreciate from my heart that I
was able to get acquainted with her in my life. Dr. Takagi was
so pleased to hear that Dr. Masako Hamada, who is an
associate professor at Villanova University, would like to
translate her book, *The Eight Female Emperors of Japan*, into
English. I can still recall her pleased expression when she
heard the news.

[From *Sakurakai,* reprinted with permission from the
55th volume of the journal of the Alumni Association
of Ochanomizu University Senior High School
(2011)]

Translators' Notes and Acknowledgements

Dr. Kiyoko Takagi was a kind and intellectual individual, who took great pleasure in sharing her knowledge with others. It is with this in mind that we have, to the best of our abilities, honored her words and intentions in our translation of her book, *The Eight Female Emperors of Japan* (*Hachinin no jotei*). Having a desire to share the deep and important history of women rulers with non-specialists, Dr. Takagi meant the book to be merely a brief introduction to the fascinating legacies of these historical figures.

Originally intended for Japanese readers, much of the culturally-specific terminology and unspoken sentiments in Dr. Takagi's writing are difficult for non-Japanese readers to understand. We have therefore endeavored to add clarity to her language where necessary and have included a limited number of footnotes to complement the text that do not appear in the original manuscript. Academic readers may find aspects of this book wanting in context and analysis, and Dr. Takagi's focus on the political and familial circumstances surrounding the female emperors reflects an attempt to compensate for their comparatively limited presence in the historical record, in spite of their undeniable importance. Furthermore, in the spirit of Dr. Takagi's desire that this glimpse into the lives of women in Japan's premodern past be

Translators' Notes and Acknowledgements 17

but a starting point for young or casual readers, we have not made extensive additions to the body of her work and have cited English-language works that students can easily consult.

The original term "*tennō*," so commonly translated as "emperor" in modern parlance, is in fact a gender-neutral term. In addition, many of the women who served as *tennō* were rulers in their own right, not necessarily endowed with the title of "empress" or wife to an emperor (as Western readers might understand the term). Therefore, in this book we have translated "*tennō*" as "female emperors" where appropriate. The poems and columns included within this volume are generously translated by Amy V. Heinrich, including those written by Dr. Takagi.

Stylistically, we have generally followed the romanization and translation conventions of the *Monumenta Nipponica* style guide, with some alterations for clarity, such as redundancies in temple names (e. g. Hōkōji Temple). Dates are given according to the premodern Japanese lunar calendar. They begin with the era name, followed by the lunar month, followed by the day. We have supplemented the Western date (e.g. Hōreki 13 (1763).11.27).

Our deepest gratitude goes to Kikuko Sakamoto, President of Fuzambo International for making this project possible, and to Richard Showstack for his dedicated work as editor. Any errors in translation are our own.

Introduction

Translated by Amy V. Heinrich

The Existence of Female Emperors

After Princess Toshinomiya Aiko (b. 2001) turned three, the question of female emperors *jotei*, today called female emperors (*josei tennō*), became an issue to be grappled with in earnest in Japanese society. On the one hand, this issue is a matter of future imperial succession. On the other, it also raises the more general question as to whether or not, in the twenty-first century, when we are moving from a male-centered society to one with equal rights for men and women, Japan can have a female emperor.

According to current Imperial Household Law, imperial succession is limited to male members of the imperial family. For the elevation of a woman emperor to occur, these policies must be revised. The subject of gender parity in the imperial line is not merely idle speculation, for Japan has only been without a female emperor in its modern history. Prior to the birth of Prince Hisahito in 2006, the imperial line consisted of only female relatives, leading to apprehension in Japanese society regarding imperial succession. Based on this concern, in January of 2005, the Prime Minister established a private advisory group, the "Advisory Council on Imperial Household Law." The first meeting of the ten committee members was held on January 25, and initial steps were taken towards a revision of the Imperial Household Law that would allow for the tenability of present-day female emperors. With Hisahito's birth, however, the proposal was dropped.

Outside these imperial lineage deliberations, the word *jotei* has been used with a completely different meaning. Though not as common in recent years, newspapers and weekly magazines used the term *jotei* to refer to a strong-minded woman, one who featured prominently in public discussion. Whether referring to the wife of a foreign president or a CEO of a large corporation, *jotei* was used to negatively describe a woman who leverages the power of her husband's position, goes to great lengths to be heard, and who desires more influence. Why and when the word *jotei* began to be used in this way is unclear, but the use of the term to disparage women has tarnished the respect due to the actual female emperors of Japan.

Although it may not be common knowledge, in Japan's history, there have been eight female emperors whose rules spanned ten imperial reigns. The reason the word *jotei* came into later use instead of *tennō* is not clear, but the practice of calling female emperors *jotei* seems to have derived from Heian period (794-1185) examples, including the well-known epic *A Tale of Flowering Fortunes* (*Eiga monogatari*). The

Introduction

word may have emerged from adding the character for "woman," 女 to the term "emperor," 帝 (*mikado*), customarily used for a male emperor; a female *mikado* thus became female emperor, that is, *jotei* 女帝.[1]

The ten reigns of female emperors, given in the traditional order, are as follows. The ancient emperors: Emperor Suiko (33rd), Emperor Kōgoku (35th), Emperor Saimei (37th), Emperor Jitō (41st), Emperor Genmei (43rd), Emperor Genshō (44th), Emperor Kōken (46th), and Emperor Shōtoku (48th). A great deal of time passed between the reign of Shōtoku and that of the next female emperors in the early modern period, Emperor Meishō (109th) and Emperor Go-Sakuramachi (117th). The title "Emperor So-and-so" was a posthumous name or title. Both Emperors Kyōgoku and Saimei of the Asuka period (538 to 710) and Emperors Kōken and Shōtoku of the Nara period (710-794) were women enthroned twice under different names. Exempting emperors whose reigns are considered to be mythological, the ten reigns of the eight female emperors make up almost ten percent of all emperors, which is no small number. It is well-known that the female emperors were enthroned after the deaths of their husbands, the previous emperors, or as princesses who served as intermediaries until a prince reached

---

[1] In the past, the term *jotei* 女帝 was also pronounced *nyotei*.

maturity. This was a necessity for the continuance of the emperor's line. Even so, there is something more to be said of that necessity and the importance of women to the continuity of the imperial house.

Since the titles of these female emperors as Emperor So-and-so (So-and-so *tennō*) are posthumous and the character for "woman" was not used in historical documents of the time, it is not immediately clear from the characters used to write their names that the female emperors were, in fact, female. Although some of the female emperors from the Nara period, such as Emperor Suiko or Emperor Jitō, may be familiar to Japanese people from the history they learned in school, there are many people who do not know from their names alone that there were two female emperors in the Tokugawa period. If we consider foreign examples, Queen Elizabeth is the current English monarch—that is, "Queen," not "King." In Holland, Denmark, and other places, there have been a number of queens in recent years. Emperors in Japan still cannot be identified as either male or female from just their titles. Linguistically speaking, an emperor is thus an emperor, a status that transcends male and female gender divisions.

It is unclear why the enthronements of the eight female emperors were limited to the ancient and early modern periods, with an 800-year gap in between. This may have been related to the frequency of male child emperors with

Introduction   *23*

strong male regents present in later centuries,[2] or because
there was, particularly in the Asuka and Nara periods, some
significance to enthroning female emperors. One key may be
the age of female emperors' enthronement throughout the
Nara period. The approximate age of each female emperor
was as follows: Emperor Suiko, 39; Kyōgoku, 49; Saimei,
62; Jitō, 42; Genmei, 47; Genshō, 36; Kōken, 32; and
Shōtoku, 47. Even excluding the twice-enthroned Emperors
Saimei and Shōtoku, those were fairly advanced ages for the
time.[3] These are also unusually high ages for male emperors.
Emperor Kōken was 32 years old, comparatively young, when
she went from crown prince to emperor.

There are only two examples of emperors reascending
the throne after abdication, and both of them were female
emperors of the Asuka and Nara periods respectively.
Emperor Kōgyoku, who abdicated during the Taika Reform,
became Emperor Saimei two reigns later, and Emperor
Kōken, after one reign, reascended the throne as Emperor

---

[2] Throughout Japan's history, there have been many examples of
successive emperors who were enthroned before reaching ten years
of age or while in their teens. There are even cases of two or three-
year olds being enthroned, and, in such cases, it is clear that they
existed as emperors in name only while a regent (*kanpaku* 関白),
the person of authority at the time, held actual power.

[3] These ages are given in the traditional Japanese way of counting
age, in which a baby in considered one-year old at birth.

Shōtoku. Emperors were not "one era-one reign" until the end of the Tokugawa period, and, before then, there were many examples of enthronement changes caused by political maneuvering. In the case of men, imperial succession was presumed to pass from father to eldest son, but, in actuality, there were fierce contests over the throne among brothers, uncles, and nephews. Especially in eras such as the Fujiwara regency and *Insei* period during the Heian period,[4] or when the bakufu (warrior government) was vying for power, people of authority other than the emperor himself manipulated the imperial institution and struggled to install someone from their own families as emperor. In other words, in the case of male successors, re-enthronement was seldom considered. But for female emperors, re-enthronement did occur, and entailed the same justification used for protecting male succession; it

---

[4] During the Heian period, the Fujiwara were one of several powerful families involved in court government. They strategically acquired high-ranking positions and utilized marriage politics (establishing Fujiwara women as imperial wives and consorts) to become fathers and grandfathers to offspring of the imperial family. Using these positions, they maintained considerable power behind the throne. Similarly, during this same period, emperors attempted to retain influence over politics by taking the tonsure (becoming a monk) and retiring at a young age, able to exert more influence over court politics from behind the scenes after abdication. This process was known as the *insei* (cloistered rule) system.

was a kind of "overtime" established in order to install one's own family member as emperor. This pattern will be discussed more concretely in the chapters that follow.

Although historically speaking there were eight female emperors, in the premodern Japanese histories, the *Kojiki* and *Nihon shoki* (*Nihongi*), two other female figures appear as imperial authorities of significant power: the famous Empress Jingū and the little-known Emperor Iitoyo. Because they appear during the mythic "Age of the Gods," the veracity of their existence cannot be confirmed, but their stories are nevertheless described below.

The Story of Empress Jingū

Today, Empress Jingū is not considered to have actually existed, but in the *Kojiki* and the *Nihon shoki* she is described as empress to the 14th emperor, Emperor Chūai (r. c. 192-200). Although it is now believed that authorities in the Nara period created the myth of Empress Jingū for their own reasons, her legend is unusually vivid and powerful for a female sovereign. Better known by her posthumous name, Empress Jingū, in the *Nihon shoki*, Jingū was first called Okinaga Tarashihime.[5] The name may sound unusual today, but the Okinaga were a powerful family in their time and an influential lineage in the ancient court. Tarashihime was said to be beautiful and wise by nature, and she filled her father with wonder. She later became empress and accompanied Emperor Chūai to Anato in Nagato province (now Toyoura in Yamaguchi prefecture) in order to subjugate the Kumaso, a powerful lineage that held power in the southern Kyushu area. From there, they crossed to Tsukushi. While staying at Kashii Shrine, Empress Jingū received an oracle from the *kami* (spirit or deity) Sumiyoshi. The message said, "The Kumaso are worthless and not worth attacking. But across the sea there is the land of Shiragi,[6] which is rich in wealth and treasures. If you offer me many prayers, that land will surrender. And, naturally, the Kumaso will submit as well..." However, the Emperor Chūai doubted the words of the *kami*. He climbed a nearby hill and gazed over the sea, but did not see a trace of Shiragi's shores. The emperor criticized the *kami*, and the *kami* once more descended to the empress and censured Chūai. In the end, the emperor ignored the divine will, and though he attacked the Kumaso, he was defeated and turned back. In the following year, he died suddenly, and this was believed to be because he disobeyed the will of the *kami*.

---

[5] "Okinaga" is written in the *Nihon shoki* with the characters 息長 or 気長.

[6] Shiragi (romanized in English as Silla) was one of the three ancient Korean kingdoms, the others being Kōkuri (Goguryeo) and Kudara (Baekje).

Introduction

Empress Jingū resolved to hide the emperor's death, to worship the god he had cursed, and to conquer Shiragi; she entered the sacred Itsuki no miya dwelling,[7] had her chief retainer, Takenouchi no Sukune, play the koto, and was possessed by the *kami*. The empress, possessed by the will of the *kami*, then proceeded to Shiragi. There are many famous episodes recorded about the Jingū's journey to Shiragi, such as her fishing at Matsuura, but most well-known is that the empress, dressed as a man, entered Shiragi and quickly subjugated it, turning Shiragi into a tributary state. Upon hearing this, the neighboring state, Kudara, also began to pay tribute. Having achieved her goals, Jingū returned home. She had been pregnant during the invasion and safely delivered a son, who was to become the later Emperor Ōjin (r. c. 270-310).

Legends surrounding Ōjin's birth have also been transmitted since ancient times. Empress Jingū, who was pregnant at the time Emperor Chūai died, purportedly announced that the child she was carrying would rule the land. In the midst of the Shiragi conquest, Jingū went into labor. However, by putting rocks against her belly, Jingū was able to delay the birth until her return to Tsukushi (Kyushu).

---

[7] Itsuki no miya was a residence intended for the imperial princess serving in the ceremonial role of high priestess for Ise Shrine.

The stones, said to be miraculous in nature, were called *chinkaiseki*, literally "quieting embrace stones." [8]

Taking the prince, Jingū returned to the capital. They are said to have encountered various difficulties on their journey home, but each time, assisted by the strength of the *kami*, Jingū overcame them. In Iware in Asuka, she built the Wakazakura Shrine for her son, known then as Prince Hondawake, who then became crown prince. Even afterwards, as Empress Dowager, Jingū managed state affairs for a period spanning forty-seven years. During that time, the crown prince never ascended the throne, so, in essence, Jingū carried out an emperor's duties.

Whether or not the story of Empress Jingū is a legend or reality, several points are of interest. For one, the empress was often possessed; she was what was later seen as a "spirit medium," and this has been considered by some scholars to be a special feature of emperors, particularly female emperors. [9]

---

[8] The *Man'yōshū* contains a poem by Yamanoue no Okura on the subject [MYS 5.813].

[9] Scholarship has long recognized that early female rulers and chieftains were recorded as having spiritual or shamanic abilities. This is not, however, to the exclusion of men, and it should be recognized that male emperors also served as leaders with connections to the spiritual world. See Joan R. Piggott, *The Emergence of Japanese Kingship* (Stanford: Stanford University Press, 1997), 26-28, 39-40.

But this tale was likely not the sole creation of the writers of the *Nihon shoki*. If we assume it was written based on myths that had been handed down, the perpetuation of the Jingū mythology might have been a useful way to historically situate the character of female emperors up to the Nara period. Finally, that Empress Jingū continued to govern after the prince was born, preserving her own child's place as emperor, is an occurrence often seen among the later female emperors. In this sense, the legend of Empress Jingū may have been a model for actual female emperors. Although Empress Jingū was technically an empress and her story is perhaps more legendary than factual, in the medieval historical treatise *Gukanshō,* written by the priest Jien and thought to be based on the *Nihon shoki,* Jien counted Empress Jingū as the fifteenth emperor. The historical tale *Mizukagami* also mentions Empress Jingū and her era, saying that "female emperors began at this time."

The Story of Emperor Iitoyo

While the story of Empress Jingū appears more mythological in nature, that of Emperor Iitoyo is imbued with a sense of reality. In the *Kojiki* and the *Nihon shoki*, she is treated as an emperor, including an annotation that even says she was the first female emperor. Her tale begins with the lineage of Emperor Yūryaku (r. c. 456-479). There is a strong

30

possibility that Emperor Yūryaku (the 21st emperor) was real, and his supposed heroics are treated in detail in ancient historical texts, including the belief that he may correspond to King Wu of the Five Kings of Yamato referred to the Chinese Song Dynasty Histories. Emperor Yūryaku is also thought to be the ruler referred to on a sword unearthed at the Inariyama tomb as "Great King." There are a great many anecdotes about Yūryaku, who may have actually been one of the founders of the Yamato state. The fact that the first poem in the *Man'yōshū* — "Your basket, with your pretty basket"—is ascribed to Emperor Yūryaku is significant.

Emperor Yūryaku's third child became the next emperor, Emperor Seinei (r. c. 480-484). However, this emperor was unremarkable and his accession to the throne was more like a coup d'état.[10] After his enthronement, the court sought out imperial successors and set their sights on two princes in Harima province, Prince Oke and Prince Woke, who were both were grandsons of the seventeenth emperor, Emperor Richū (r. c. 400-405). The emperor welcomed these two princes, making the elder crown prince and the younger imperial prince, but soon after, Emperor Seinei died. It was only natural for the older brother, Crown Prince Oke, to ascend to the throne as the next emperor. However, for

---

[10] He was also known as Emperor Shirakami, literally, "Emperor White-hair," as he supposedly had white hair from birth.

Introduction   *31*

whatever reason, Oke tried to abdicate in favor of his younger brother, but Woke did not accept it. Both the brothers conceded the imperial throne to each other, and the matter remained unresolved. It was then that the brothers' older sister (some say younger sister and some say aunt) Iitoyo entered the picture. Under these circumstances, Iitoyo ascended the throne. The *Nihon shoki* states this about the matter:

> In the spring of the fifth year, in the first month, Emperor Shirakami [Emperor Seinei] passed away. That month, Crown Prince Oke and the Emperor both renounced the throne. For a time, there was no emperor. Because of this, the Princess Irone Iitoyo no Aonohima miko was enthroned at Oshinumi no Tsunosashi no miya. She called herself Emperor Oshinumi no Iitoyo no Ao. A poet of the time composed the following:
>
> In Yamato what I long to see -
> The high stronghold of Oshinumi
> The palace of Tsunosashi!

yamato be ni / miga hoshi mono wa / oshinumi no/
          kono takaki naru / tsunosashi no miya

Emperor Iitoyo, who took the throne, died in the eleventh

32

month of the same year, so she was only emperor for a very short period. But references to her in ancient histories such as the *Fusōryakuki* say, "Emperor Iitoyo, the twenty-fourth reign," and the *Kōin shōunroku* states, "Emperor Iitoyo is the female king of Oshinumi," thus presenting her as emperor. In Jien's *Gukanshō*, as well, for the time of Emperor Ninken (r. c. 488-498), it states, "... The siblings' *jotei* was established. She was named Emperor Iitoyo. She ascended the throne in the second month and died in the eleventh month. This was omitted in the chronicles of imperial reigns..."

Emperor Iitoyo thus differs from Empress Jingū. She is seen in histories as someone who served as an intermediary emperor, rather than standing out politically or diplomatically. Moreover, other writings on Iitoyo in the *Nihon shoki* also suggest she had a shaman-like character. The existence of this female emperor, surprisingly unknown except by historians, was a herald of the appearance of later female emperors in history.

The *Nihon shoki* also stated that when the future Emperor Kinmei (the 29th emperor, r. 539-571) was to be enthroned but found to be too young, there was a request that the former Empress Yamada, his mother, become emperor. However, she declined on the grounds that, as a woman, she was unqualified. This story suggests that not only was it commonly believed that the throne should not be vacant for even a day, but also that in spite of the prevalence of female emperors in history and legend, some people, likely influenced by Confucian precepts asserting male superiority, believed that a woman was an inappropriate choice for emperor. Even so, the female rulers that followed after Kinmei's time performed the role of emperor with great diligence and ability.

Column 1

There was Almost a Female Emperor in the Last Years of the Heian Period

In the late Heian period, Emperor Konoe (r. 1142-1155) died at age sixteen, and there was no prince to succeed him. The next emperor was expected to be Prince Masahito, the younger brother of Retired Emperor Sutoku (r. 1123-1142), but there were issues surrounding his conduct, so instead, the names of three other people were put forth: Emperor Konoe's younger sister, Princess Shōshi, Retired Emperor Sutoku's first son, Prince Shigehito, and Prince Masahito's child, Prince Morohito. The debate over who should be selected lasted through the night until the following morning, but, in the end, Prince Masahito was selected, and he was enthroned as Emperor Go-Shirakawa (r. 1155-1158). Princess Shōshi was seventeen at the time. At the age of twenty-one, she became a nun and was called "Hachijō-in." This event is seen not only in the Tendai Abbot Jien's *Gukanshō*, but is described in *setsuwa* (medieval short story) collections such as *Ima kagami* and *Kojidan*. If Princess Shōshi had ascended the throne, the history of female emperors may well have been different.

Emperor Suiko
(r. 592-628)

Translated by Masako Hamada

*The female emperor on the throne for thirty-six
years who worked closely with Prince Shōtoku.*

Princess Nukatabe

Emperor Suiko, also known as Princess Nukatabe, was
the first female emperor of Japan. That in and of itself makes
her role in Japanese history very significant. Emperor Suiko
was born in 544 as the second daughter of the twenty-ninth
Emperor Kinmei. She was called Princess Nukatabe as well as
Princess Toyomike Kashigiya. Emperor Kinmei had six
consorts (of *hi* and *bunin* status),[11] and the fourth (a daughter
of Cabinet Minister Soga no Iname no Sukune), Princess
Kitashi, had seven sons and six daughters. The oldest son was
Tachibana no Toyohi mikoto, who became Emperor Yōmei
(r. 585-587), and the fourth daughter was Princess Toyomike

---

[11] For more information on consort status, see Column 3.

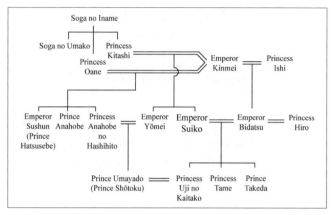

Lineage of Emperor Suiko

Kashigiya, which meant that the thirty-first Emperor Yōmei and Emperor Suiko had the same mother. In that era, a child's future was influenced not only by their father's background, but also their mother's. Emperors Yōmei and Suiko were both grandchildren of a very influential man, Soga no Iname, a fact which helped them politically in their lives. Princess Nukatabe was described in *Nihon shoki* as a "beautiful lady with elegant manners," and she was a woman gifted with both loveliness and intelligence. Even if the *Nihon shoki* described her in flattering terms, it is clear she was no ordinary princess. When she was eighteen years old, Nukatabe married Emperor Bidatsu (r. 572-585) and became empress. Emperor Bidatsu was the second son of Emperor Kinmei, and succeeded him to the throne. He did not accept Buddhism, which had just

Emperor Suiko 37

recently been introduced into Japan, but enjoyed poetry. Four years after his enthronement, Bidatsu made Princess Hiro, a daughter of Prince Okinaga no mate, his empress, but, unfortunately, she died shortly thereafter. The following year, he made Princess Nukatabe (who was in fact his half-sister) his new empress. They had two sons and five daughters. One of the princesses, Uji no Kaitako, became consort of Prince Shōtoku,[12] while Princess Tame became the empress of Emperor Jomei (r. 629-641). It was not unusual to have consanguineous marriage at that time. While it was prohibited to marry one's own brother or sister from the same parents, consanguineous marriage by other connections was an important factor in establishing one's own political sphere of influence.

During Emperor Bidatsu's reign, there were no major incidents, but the *Nihon shoki* records various interactions with what is now the Korean peninsula, such as travel to and from the kingdoms of Koma, Shiragi, and Kudara, and the reconstruction of Mimana, another Korean state, which had been recently destroyed by Shiragi. Though disputed in scholarship, Mimana is thought to have once been a direct

---

[12] Although Shōtoku was crown prince, he is conventionally identified in scholarship as "Prince Shōtoku," and is so labeled here.

holding of the Japanese imperial family, a territory that they endeavored to recover.

Buddhism, which was brought into Japan from Kudara during the rule of Emperor Kinmei, was also introduced from Shiragi. Soga no Umako (c. 551-626), the son of Soga no Iname and a powerful person in the court, had ardently embraced Buddhist faith for some time and focused on using his influence to build Buddhist temples and statues. In contrast, Moriya of the Mononobe clan, which opposed the Soga, rejected Buddhism, and the conflict between them was unceasing. While this was a religious dispute, it was also one over political power. The conflict came to a head when Emperor Bidatsu died unexpectedly. Although Emperor Bidatsu died from illness, the Mononobe clan blamed his death on the Soga, claiming that they had neglected the worship of the native *kami* (spirits) in favor of the foreign religion, Buddhism. The discord between them only deepened. Prince Anahobe (Emperor Kinmei's son), who had been hoping to ascend to the imperial throne for some time, observed the situation between the Soga and the Mononobe from the sidelines.

The First Female Emperor

Prince Tachibana no Toyohi (Princess Kashigiya's older brother) was crowned emperor after the death of Emperor Bidatsu. He became the thirty-first emperor, Emperor Yōmei. He built a palace at Asuka iware and his rule began. Just as in the previous reign, Soga no Umako was made Cabinet Minister (*oo'omi*), and Mononobe no Moriya was made Chief Minister (*oomuraji*). The following year, Emperor Yōmei made Princess Anahobe no Hashihito his empress, and she bore him four sons. The first boy was Prince Umayado, who became Prince Shōtoku (574-622). Princess Kashigiya (the future Emperor Suiko) and Prince Shōtoku were therefore aunt and nephew.

To return to the subject of the emperor, there was an incident on the occasion of Emperor Bidatsu's death. Prince Anahobe, who, as previously noted, aimed to ascend to the imperial throne, tried to rape Princess Kashigiya, who was mourning in the temporary mortuary of her late husband, Emperor Bidatsu. Anahobe was subdued by Miwa no kimi Sakashi, Emperor Bitastu's favored retainer. Angered that Miwa no kimi Sakashi had attacked the princess, Prince Anahobe retaliated with the aid of Umako and Moriya. Sakashi managed to escape, but he was later killed by a retainer of the prince. A series of insults exchanged between Umako and Moriya during this incident only intensified their political power struggle.

Their conflict over Buddhism worsened the situation, and it reached its peak when Emperor Yōmei fell ill and said that he wanted to devote himself to Buddhism. Moriya opposed the emperor's desire, saying that his illness was caused by his neglect of the rituals of the native *kami* and his belief in foreign deities. Umako, on the other hand, said that he himself would become a Buddhist monk if the Emperor's illness worsened, but the Emperor soon passed away. The section on Emperor Yōmei in the *Nihon shoki* discusses this incident but little else was written about domestic affairs and diplomatic matters. In the shadow of the power struggle between the influential Soga and Mononobe clans, Emperor Yōmei did not distinguish himself.

With the death of Emperor Yōmei, the conflict between the Soga and Mononobe reached its highest point. At first, Moriya planned to make Prince Anahobe the next emperor. However, the plan was discovered by the Soga side, and Umako placed Princess Kashigiya close to Prince Anahobe so that he could hatch a plan to assassinate him. This plan was executed shortly thereafter, and Umako then enlisted the help of other princes and ministers to destroy Moriya.

Among them was Prince Umayado, the later Prince Shōtoku. Observing this dispute, Shōtoku thought that it was possible his (Soga) clan might lose, and so he let his hair down to mark his passage to adulthood, made a statue of the

Emperor Suiko   *41*

Shitennō (the four heavenly kings of Buddhism)[13] from a
sumac tree, and vowed that if the Soga won the political battle
with the Mononobe he would build a temple dedicated to
them. The result was that Mononobe no Moriya was killed
and the Soga side won, ending the conflict. According to the
Nihon shoki, after the dispute ended, they built a Shitennō
Temple at Settsu and Hōkōji Temple at Asuka. With the end
of the Mononobe clan, Prince Hatsusebe, who supported the
Soga clan and Princess Kashigiya, was crowned as the thirty-
second Emperor Sushun (r. 587-592). Umako continued to
serve as Cabinet Minister.

Emperor Sushun was a son of Emperor Kinmei. His
mother was Oane, a daughter of Soga no Iname. Oane was a
younger sister of Princess Kitashi, mother of Princess
Kashigiya; Emperor Sushun, therefore, was Umako's nephew
and a descendent of the Soga. However, in this time period,
even if people were related by blood, they were not
necessarily close to one another; on the contrary, close blood
ties often triggered animosity and rivalry. Sushun, therefore,
did not enjoy stability in his position as emperor, given that
his uncle, Umako, held immense power in the imperial court.

---

[13] Shitennō 四天王, literally "Four Heavenly Kings," are Buddhist
deities thought to be protectors of the four directions by warding
off evil.

Notably, in the section of *Nihon shoki* concerning Emperor Sushun's reign, the first half describes the conflict between the Soga and the Mononobe, while in the latter half, only one entry describes the politics surrounding Sushun. In this incident, it is said that a wild boar was presented to the emperor. When the emperor saw the boar, he commented, "Someday I would like to cut off the head of a person who I hate just as I shall cut off the head of this wild boar." He prepared his army for war, perhaps in preparation for such an event. After hearing this story, Umako thought that Sushun despised him and planned to have the emperor assassinated. On a day when the emperor was receiving tribute from the Tōgoku region, he was murdered by Azuma no Aya no Ataikoma at Umako's bidding. Azumano no Aya no Ataikoma was later put to death for having had a relationship with Kawakami no Iratsume, who was the emperor's consort. Since Emperor Kinmei's time, a number of emperors were heavily influenced by the power of the Soga clan. As a result, they left no outstanding political legacies, and were manipulated by individuals like Umako. In particular, Emperor Sushun, who lost his life to Umako despite his innocence, was remembered only as an emperor who was assassinated by his subordinate. Emperor Suiko was crowned the first female emperor after this major incident.

The Crowning of the First Female Emperor

After the sudden death of Emperor Sushun, there was chaos surrounding who would be the next emperor. The best candidate was Emperor Bidatsu's crown prince, Prince Oshisaka no Hikohito no Ooe, but he was in poor health and was not enthroned. There is also a theory that he had already passed away. Prince Takeda, the son of Emperor Bidatsu and Princess Kashigiya, was still too young. Another possibility was Prince Umayado, who was nineteen years old and a son of Emperor Yōmei. Any one of these individuals could have become emperor, but the *Nihon shoki* does not give any details on the decision-making process. For Soga no Umako, who held the actual political power in court, which of the candidates was chosen was irrelevant, since all of the princes were connected to him by blood. Princess Kashigiya wanted her beloved son, Prince Takeda, to succeed to the throne, but her ministers requested that she become the next emperor. The empress twice firmly refused to become the emperor, but she acquiesced after she was asked for a third time.

With this, the first female emperor was enthroned. She is now known as Emperor Suiko. Once before, at the time of Emperor Kinmei's succession to the throne, Empress Kasuga no Yamada, wife of the twenty-seventh emperor, Emperor Ankan (r. 531-536), was asked to succeed to the throne, but she refused to accept the position on the grounds that it was not a duty a woman should be entrusted with. It is not known if Princess Kashigiya also believed this to be so. She might have accepted the position thinking that she could pass the throne to her son, Prince Takeda, when he came of age, but no doubt Umako's desires also had an influence. Another reason the ministers recommended that she become emperor was that there was a need to have a shamanistic maiden as an officiating priestess paying homage to the *kami*. It was believed that Emperor Suiko, as a female, was endowed with such shamanistic power.[14]

Emperor Suiko was thirty-nine years old when she succeeded to the throne at Toyura no miya in the twelfth month of 592. As with other emperors, the appellation "Emperor Suiko" was established after her death; at the time of her rule, she was called Emperor Toyomike Kashigiya.

Emperor Suiko appointed Prince Umayado as crown prince and trusted him with all political matters. For all intents and purposes, it appeared as if Suiko and Umayado were acting under joint rulership. However, in fact, Soga no Umako was in control of the regime under the guise of assisting them. Emperor Suiko's administration thus operated under the regency of Crown Prince Umayado (Prince Shōtoku).

---

[14] See footnote 9.

Emperor Suiko   45

In domestic political affairs, the major accomplishments of the era were the establishment of twelve ranks in the imperial court, the creation of the Seventeen Article Constitution, and the compilation of an imperial history. A great deal of effort was also put into promoting Buddhism. Furthermore, diplomacy and exchange prospered with the Korean kingdoms Shiragi, Kudara, Koma, and Mimana. Among the exchanges were Buddhist monks visiting the Yamato state, particularly from Shiragi, which was powerful at the time. Armies had also been sent to recapture Mimana, and though they had only reached the island of Tsukushi, they returned to Yamato in Suiko 3 (595). When an envoy was dispatched to Shiragi two years later, in return, Shiragi sent the emperor two magpies and one peacock as tribute. Kudara also sent a camel, a donkey, two sheep and one pheasant. There is no record in the *Nihon shoki* of how they raised the camel, but it must have been a shock for the people of that time to see one!

In Suiko 8 (600), the imperial court dispatched troops to Shiragi again. Over 10,000 soldiers crossed the ocean under the leadership of generals and commanders. The invasion was successful and the government of Shiragi surrendered four castles and their surrounding regions to Yamato. They were located in a central region of Mimana that was believed by the Yamato court to have formerly been Yamato imperial territory. Despite this victory, the court once again dispatched

46

an expeditionary force. However, Prince Kume, younger brother of Prince Shōtoku and a general at the time, died of illness. His successor, Prince Tagima (a half-brother to Prince Shōtoku) abandoned their plans after his wife, who was accompanying him on the venture, passed away. After this, Yamato's relationship with Shiragi continued in various forms.

In Suiko 15 (607), the imperial court sent Ono no Imoko to China. In *Nihon shoki,* the name of this country is written as "Daitōkoku," which we now know to be part of today's China. At the time, China was under the rule of the Sui Dynasty (581-618). This mission was one of the greatest successes in the state's administration: it showed Yamato's grand intention to have diplomatic relations with a major kingdom in Asia other than those of the Korean Peninsula. It is written in Sui dynasty histories that the Chinese emperor, Emperor Yōdai (r. 604-618),[15] was angry that they, a very prosperous nation, had received a sovereign letter requesting equal diplomatic relations from a "barbarian nation" like Yamato. Imoko returned to Japan in the fourth month of the following year along with the diplomat Haiseisei (Pei Shiqing), who was sent as an envoy on behalf of the Sui.

---

[15] In English, Emperor Yang (569-618), the second Sui dynasty ruler.

Imoko went to the Sui again in the ninth month along with Takamuku no Kuromaro, Minabuchi no Shōan, and a priest named Min, all of whom had gone to China for study. They were members of the next generation that later played an important role in international and religious relations. Yamato's diplomatic connection with the Sui dynasty thus had a significant impact on Japan's domestic and international development.

One of the most notable things to happen during Emperor Suiko's reign was the proliferation of Buddhism. Emperor Bidatsu, Emperor Suiko's husband, was not fond of the religion, though in the face of Buddhism's popularity at the time, his attitude was quite passive. Soga no Umako, on the other hand, accepted Buddhism wholly, and, Suiko's blood connection with the Soga notwithstanding, she was also very much interested in Buddhism.

According to the *Nihon shoki*, in the first month of the first year of her enthronement, Emperor Suiko placed a bone supposedly belonging to the Buddha in the pillar foundation stone of the temple Hōkōji (Asukadera) while it was under construction. From the start, Hōkōji was a large-scale construction project and took many years. It was finally completed in the eleventh month of Suiko 4 (596). Emperor Suiko also built the temple Arahaka (Shitennōji) in Naniwa, and, in the second month of Suiko 2 (594), she issued an imperial edict commanding the crown prince and ministers to promote the Three Treasures (Buddha, the Dharma, and Buddhist monks) as a means to make the land more prosperous. This might have been at the behest of Prince Shōtoku, but we can see the faith of Emperor Suiko behind the order as well. Because of the edict, the imperial ministers competed to build houses (which later came to be referred to as temples) for the worship of Buddha.

Monks from Koma and Kudara also often visited Japan. One of the monks from Koma, Eji, became Prince Shōtoku's teacher. Eji and another monk from Kudara named Esō were tasked with spreading Buddhism. Not only monks, but also images of the Buddha and sutra (Buddhist scriptures) were brought in, and it was necessary to build temples to hold the icons. The temple Hachiokadera was said to have been built by the legendary figure Hata no Kawakatsu[16] at the request of Prince Shōtoku, and though the location is different, this was the predecessor of the present-day Kōryūji (Uzumasaji).

In Suiko 11 (603), Emperor Suiko relocated the capital to

---

[16] Hata no Kawakatsu was an early seventh-century figure and leader of the Hata family. Dedicated to Buddhism, he was a close advisor and supporter of Prince Shōtoku. Many legends surround Kawakatsu, including that he performed dramatic pieces at Shōtoku's behest to quell political unrest, a style of entertainment that would develop into the popular theatrical practice *sarugaku* 猿楽.

Emperor Suiko

Asuka Oharida, but, two years later, Prince Shōtoku moved
the residence to the much more distant Ikaruga no miya.
Hōryuji Temple was built there, and Buddhist activities
continued to proliferate. One such project was the creation of
a Buddha statue made of copper. The builders planned to
enshrine it in the main hall of Gankōji Temple, but the statue
was too large. However, the famous artisan Kuratsukuri no
tori (better known as Tori busshi) was able to install the statue
inside the temple without breaking the door. The emperor
therefore issued a proclamation praising his family[17] and
awarded him gifts. It is also said that from this time, the
kanbutsu-e ceremony (to celebrate the birthday of Buddha)
began to be conducted on the eighth day of the fourth month
and *urabon* ceremonies (to pray for one's ancestors who have
passed away) were conducted on the fifteenth day of the
seventh month.

The reading of Buddhist sutras, which accompanied the
numerous imported Buddha statues, also often occurred.
According to *Nihon shoki*, in the fall of the fourteenth year of
Emperor Suiko's reign (606), she also had Prince Shōtoku

---

[17] Specifically, the emperor praised the deeds of Kuratsukuri no
tori and his father, Shiba Tatto, who was a Chinese immigrant.
According to the *Nihon shoki*, in the late sixth century, Shiba Tatto
assisted Soga no Umako to find practitioners of Buddhism in
Japan.

50

lecture on a text called *Shōmangyō* (which contained three annotated commentaries on important Buddhist sutras), and he completed the task over the course of three days. Shōtoku's achievements were also written about in early biographies of Shōtoku, titled *Shōgū Shōtoku hōōtei setsu* and *Hōryuji engi shizaichō*.[18] In 606, Shōtoku also lectured on another text, the Lotus Sutra. There are no official records of any transcriptions of the Vimalakirti sutra (*yuima-kyō*), but it later became famous as *Shōtoku no sangyōgisho* (*Shōtoku's Annotated Commentaries on the Three Sutras*). Some, however, theorize that the *Sangyōgisho* may be a forgery.

There were many individuals who came from Koma, Kudara and China to promote the practice of Buddhism. Emperor Suiko, Prince Shōtoku, and Soga no Umako all had a deep faith in Buddhism and, with their support, the number of Buddhist temples, statues, and monks increased. This created the foundation of Buddhism in Japan. According to a document from Suiko 32 (624), as a result of their efforts, forty-six temples were built, 816 men became monks, and 569 women became nuns (a combined total of 1,385). The second article of Prince Shōtoku's Seventeen Article Constitution stated that "sincere reverence will be given to the Three

---

[18] These are not part of *Nihon shoki*, but are separate biographies of Shōtoku.

Treasures, which are Buddha, the dharma, and Buddhist monks," and those goals gradually came to fruition.

Not only was Buddhism brought in from other countries, but texts on Confucianism, a calendar system, and the study of astronomy, geology, and astrology were also introduced. Chinese medicine was introduced during the T'ang Dynasty (618-907), and the number of students studying Chinese medicine in Japan increased. Also, traditional *gigaku*[19] music was brought to Japan from from Kudara.

In *Nihon shoki*, there is a record of the public works projects undertaken during Emperor Suiko's reign. In Suiko 15 (607) Takechi Pond, Fujiwara Pond, Kataoka Pond, and Sugahara Pond were developed in Yamato province, and a large moat was built in Kurikoma, Yamashiro province. Other ponds, such as Togari Pond and Yosami Pond, were created in Kawachi province. Ponds mentioned in *Nihon shoki* include Mitake Pond, Yamada Pond and Kama Pond. In Suiko 21 (613), Ekigami Pond, Unebi Pond, and Wani Pond were created. The reason so many ponds were established was for the irrigation of rice fields, which demonstrated the government's interest in furthering the development of agriculture. Also, *miyake* (storehouses located on land directly

---

[19] *Gigaku* 伎楽 is genre of masked dance performance introduced to Japan in the Asuka period (538-710).

controlled by the imperial court) were placed in each province, and *mibube* (imperial offices) were also created to financially support the upbringing of princes and princesses. In addition, a main road was built running from Naniwa to Asuka, a street that still exists as the Takeuchi Highway. A private road may have also been built for Prince Shōtoku to commute from his residence in Ikaruga to the capital in Asuka. This commuting road was likely necessary for political reasons.

Articles in *Nihon shoki* from after Suiko 21 (613) touch on other issues, such as statecraft and diplomacy. One was *kusurigari*, an event held on the fifth day of the fifth month of Suiko 19 (611) and 22 (614), in which the ears of deers were collected and dried to be used as a medicinal tonic. In Suiko 24 (616), even though it was only the first month of the year, peach and pear trees bore fruit, and in Izumo province, melons in the shape of earthenware teapots grew. In Suiko 27 (619), a strange creature that was said to be neither a fish nor a person was caught in a fisherman's net in Settsu province, and, in the following year, a red shape over three meters wide that resembled a pheasant was seen in the sky. These strange occurrences were considered omens that Prince Shōtoku (then forty-nine years old) would soon die, and he indeed did pass away in Suiko 29 (621 or 622, according some theories). According to *Nihon shoki,* people of all ranks and status expressed their sadness: "The light is gone from the sun and

Emperor Suiko   53

the moon and they have fallen from the heavens. From now
on, who can we depend on?"

With Prince Shōtoku governing as regent, Emperor
Suiko had been overshadowed and seldom seen, but her voice
can be heard in several places in *Nihon shoki*. For example,
on Suiko 20 (612).1.7, she held a banquet with her ministers,
at which Cabinet Minister Soga no Umako offered a
celebratory poem. In concert with his words, Emperor Suiko
continued the poem by adding:

The glorious Sogas!
The children of the Sogas,
were they horses,
would be mounts of Himuka;
were they swords,
would be fine blades of Kure!
Indeed how well
the children of the Soga
serve their great lord!

masoga yo / soga no ko ra wa / uma naraba /
himuka no koma / tachi naraba /
kure no masai / ubeshi kamo / soga no ko ra o /
ookimi no / tsukawasu rashiki

[NS 106]

This poem, while praising Soga no Umako's loyalty to the emperor, expresses her joy at the success of the Soga as a member of the family herself. On the other hand, she refused a request from Umako to give him Katsuragi no Agata, a military base of the Soga, which was under direct imperial control. The emperor stated: "I am from the Soga clan and Umako is my uncle. This was a request from him, the Cabinet Minister, but accepting his request would mean losing Katsuragi no Agata. In the future, I would be called a stupid and silly woman who governed the nation, but lost Katsuragi no Agata. It would hurt my reputation and that of the Minister." She had good insight to make such a forward-thinking decision, particularly as a woman on the throne.

Umako passed away on the fifth month of Suiko 34 (626). According to the *Nihon shoki*, around this time many natural disasters occurred which, along with Umako's death, seemed to forebode the death of the emperor. At the end of the second month of Suiko 36 (628), Suiko fell ill and her condition got worse. Knowing her death was near, she tried to convince Prince Tamura, grandson of Emperor Bidatsu, to become emperor after she died. She also admonished Prince Yamashiro no Ooe, who was Shōtoku's son, saying, "You are still young. Even if you have your own ideas, you should listen to the people around you." On the seventh day of the third month of 628, Emperor Suiko, the first female emperor in Japan, passed away at the age of seventy-five when her regime was in its thirty-sixth year. Before she died, she was worried about the people who were suffering from drought, so she requested that an imperial mausoleum not be constructed for her. Instead, she requested that she be buried in the same grave as Prince Takeda, who had predeceased her. It is not hard to imagine what a blow Prince Shōtoku's death had been to Emperor Suiko. Her son, Prince Takeda, was gone, but she felt like she had lived a long life, and, from a political of point of view, contrary to expectation, she had stabilized the political circumstances of the state, if only temporarily.

Column 2

Were Emperor Suiko and Prince Takeda buried in the same tomb?

In the year 2000, the Education Committee of Kashihara City announced that two enormous stone chambers were unearthed in Ueyama, Kashihara City Nara Prefecture that rivaled even the Ishibutai tumulus[20] site thought to be the grave of Soga no Umako (*Asahi shimbun,* 8/18/2000). Judging from the time and location of construction as well as the scale, there is a strong possibility these chambers are the joint grave of Emperor Suiko and her son Prince Takeda. Emperor Suiko's mausoleum is designated by the Imperial Household Ministry as being in Taishimachi in Osaka, but it is thought that, at first, she was buried in a tomb in Ueyama with Prince Takeda in Kashihara City and later her remains were moved to the Shinaga Yamada Mausoleum in Taishimachi. While still alive, Emperor Suiko purportedly did not want to build her own tomb, but wished to be interred in the grave of her son Prince Takeda, who had died young. This discovery is thought to support that theory. The feelings of a mother, over seventy years of age, who wanted to be laid to rest in the same grave as her beloved son, are very moving.

---

[20] An artificial hillock or mound (as over a grave).

Emperor Kōgyoku

(r. 642-645)

Translated by Masako Hamada

*An emperor who was troubled by the despotism
of the Soga Clan and, after three and a half years,
was the first female emperor to abdicate the throne.*

The Second Female Emperor

Only about fifty years after Emperor Suiko's death, a
female emperor was once again enthroned. Emperor Kōgyoku
was the 35th emperor. Also known as Princess Takara and
Princess Ame no Toyotakara Ikashi Hitarasu, her father was
Prince Chinu, who was a grandson of Emperor Bitasu. Her
mother was Kibi no hime no ookimi, who was a great-grand
daughter of Emperor Kinmei.

Princess Takara was born in Suiko 2 (594) and she
became empress to Emperor Jomei, who had been enthroned
after Emperor Suiko. She gave birth to Prince Katsuragi
(better known as Prince Naka no Ooe and later Emperor
Tenji), Prince Ooama (who later became Emperor Tenmu),

and Princess Hashihito (who became empress to Emperor Kōtoku). According to another report, she was married to Prince Takamuku before marrying Emperor Jomei and gave birth to Prince Aya. This was a rare historical case in which three children of one mother became either emperor and empress, and Emperor Tenji (r. 661-672) and Emperor Tenmu (r. 673-686) were known as strong and effective emperors.

The Circumstances of Kōgyoku's Enthronement

Complicated political issues surrounded Kōgyoku's succession to the imperial throne. Emperor Suiko died seven years after the passing of the regent Prince Shōtoku, having never made a decision as to who would be the next crown prince. Before her passing, she spoke separately with both Prince Tamura (593-641) and Prince Yamashiro no Ooe (d. 643), who were both suitable candidates to ascend to the imperial throne. Although she did not name a successor, Suiko told each of them to think carefully about the future of the throne. In the end, Prince Tamura became Emperor Jomei.

There were complex reasons why Emperor Suiko did not make a decision on the next crown prince right away. Minister Soga no Emishi (the son of Umako, 587-645) had gathered the ministers to try to decide who would become the next emperor, but the ministers were split into three contending political factions— the Prince Tamura faction, the Prince Yamashiro no Ooe faction, and a neutral faction. Prior to this discussion, Emishi, who intended to put Tamura on the throne, had asked the opinion of Minister Sakaibe no Marise no Omi (a son of Soga no Umako and a younger brother of Emishi), but Sakaibe no Marise replied that he would support Prince Yamashiro no Ooe without any hesitation. Yamashiro no Ooe, who was a son of Prince Shōtoku, overheard this conversation, further fueling his existing ambitions for the throne.

When Emishi was questioned by Yamashiro no Ooe regarding the situation, Emishi did not give him direct answers. However, Yamashiro no Ooe was not deterred, and he used the late Emperor Suiko's final words to him as a pretense to continue his ambitions to become emperor. In the end, Sakaibe no Marise no Omi did support Emishi's plans and both he and Yamashiro no Ooe went into hiding in Ikaruga no miya. There, Emishi and his followers attacked and tried to killed them. Prince Yamashiro no Ooe survived the assault, but he was killed a few years later by Soga no Iruka. With this, the dispute concerning the imperial succession was over, and as Emishi's wished, Prince Tamura was enthroned as the 34th emperor, Emperor Jomei. In the first month of Jomei 2 (630), Princess Takara (who would later become Emperor Kōgyoku) was made empress.

If we take a look at the Soga family tree, Umako was a

son of Iname, who was a powerful cabinet minister and held political power during the Kinmei reign (539-571) during which, he made his daughters, Princess Kitashi and Princess Oane, consorts to the emperor. Princess Kitashi was the mother of the 31st emperor, Emperor Yōmei, and 33rd emperor, Emperor Suiko, and Princess Oane was the mother of the 32nd emperor, Emperor Sushun. Umako, who killed Emperor Sushun, was his uncle. Umako's daughter, Tojiko no Iratsume, was Prince Shōtoku's consort and the mother of Prince Yamashiro no Ooe, and another daughter, Hote no Iratsume, became consort to Prince Tamura (Emperor Jomei). As seen in this family tree, four generations of emperors from Emperor Kinmei to Emperor Jomei were all descended from the Soga clan. In control of all court politics, the Soga eliminated anyone who opposed them without mercy. The murder of Prince Yamashiro no Ooe was one example. These kinds of power struggles and rivalries among blood relatives continued throughout Japanese history.

The political era that followed the enthronement of Emperor Jomei was relatively stable. He moved to Asuka okamoto no miya in the tenth month of 630. After Asuka okamoto no miya was burned down in a fire in Jomei 8 (637), he moved to Tanaka no miya. However, Tanaka no miya was only a temporary residence. In Jomei 7 (640). 11, he announced an imperial edict to build a palace and a temple on the banks of the Kudara River (now known as the Yamato

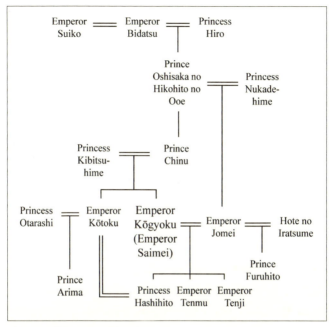

Lineage of Emperor Kōgyoku

River), which was located between Asuka and Ikaruga. He moved there the following year, but he died less than one year later. The Kudara Temple and a nine-story pagoda were built at around the same time. The fact that the Emperor Jomei had the Kudara Temple built showed that he had devoted himself to Buddhism.

Buddhism was officially brought over to Japan from Kudara during the rule of Emperor Kinmei, and Kinmei, under the protection of the Soga and patronage of Prince

Shōtoku, welcomed Buddhist monks and scripture brought to Japan. This was a time of prolific temple construction and increased Buddhist practice; Emperor Jomei, too, was personally active in and supportive of Buddhism in Japan.

This period saw active trade and exchange of Buddhist writings with foreign countries. The Sui Dynasty in China, which had a close relationship with Emperor Jomei, was overthrown in Suiko 20 (618), but was replaced by the T'ang Dynasty, with whom Jomei continued frequent contact. In Jomei 2 (630), Inugami no kimi mitasuki was dispatched as the first trade envoy to Sui from Japan. He returned home two years later with a monk, Min, along with Eon, Minabuchi no shōan, and Takamuku no kuromaro, figures who had been studying in China. They actively introduced T'ang culture to Japan and this had a tremendous influence on Japanese scholarship and Buddhism. Emperor Jomei asked Eon to lecture about the Infinite Life Sutra (muryōju-kyō).

According to Nihon shoki, the Jomei era was relatively peaceful and uneventful. During this period, the empress accompanied the emperor on a trip to the Arima hot springs in Settsu Province from the ninth month to the twelfth month of Jomei 3 (631). They stayed at Arima again from the tenth month into the new year in Jomei 10 (638) and from the twelfth month to the fourth month in Jomei 11 (639). They also stayed at a hot spring in Iyo.[21] Both the emperor and empress traveled outside the palace for three or four months a

Emperor Kōgyoku   63

year. When they returned home from Iyo, Kudara no miya was still under construction, so they moved into Umasaka no miya. Empress Takara was already forty-six years old.

Emperor Jomei passed away at Kudara no miya on Jomei 13 (641).10.9. On the eighteenth day, Prince Hirakasuwake (Prince Naka no Ooe), who was sixteen years old at the time, read messages of condolence. He was next in line of succession to be emperor, but was not considered mature enough. This led to the decision to enthrone his mother, Empress Takara. This matter was not described in *Nihon shoki*, but historians believe the precedent set by Emperor Suiko made the decision easier. Furthermore, given that there were several possible male heirs to the throne, had they not enthroned Takara, it is likely that the imperial succession crisis would have devolved into a bloody rivalry.

Both Prince Furuhito, the older half-brother of Prince Naka no Ooe, and Naka no Ooe himself were candidates. They were both sons of Emperor Jomei, but Furuhito's mother was Hote no Iratsume, a daughter of Soga no Umako, making his lineage inferior to that of Prince Naka no Ooe, whose mother was now the empress. By the time Prince

---

[21] The present day Dōgo Hot Spring, located in Matsuyama, Ehime prefecture, Dōgo is considered one of Japan's oldest and most famous hot springs.

Furuhito reached the age to succeed to the throne, he was the oldest among many imperial princes. A daughter of Prince Furuhito was consort of Prince Naka no Ooe. In addition to these two candidates, Prince Yamashiro no Ooe (who had lost the previous fight over imperial succession) was alive and well, so it was not a surprise that he tried to become the next emperor.

All three of the potential candidates were blood-related family members. The empress, who had just lost her husband, Emperor Jomei, must have wanted her son, Prince Naka no Ooe, to succeed to the throne. If she herself became the next emperor, it would be possible to pass the throne to her son when he reached maturity.

Empress Takara thus succeeded to the throne and became Emperor Ame no Toyotakara Ikasihitarasu, the 35th emperor, Emperor Kōgyōku. She was forty-nine at the time, an age that was then seen as old. Regardless of her age, much like Emperor Suiko, she became an intermediary emperor until her son's time. For Soga no Emishi, and his son, Umako, who controlled much of the court's politics, it was easy to imagine that they could manipulate this emperor.

Emperor Kōgyoku's Rule

Emperor Kōgyoku's rule lasted only three years and six months, coming to a dramatic end when the Soga clan was destroyed. The *Nihon shoki* reports on three major topics during Kōgyoku's rule: first, the despotism of the Soga; second, the relationship between Japan and the Korean peninsula; and third, terrible natural disasters. In contrast to records on Japan's relatively uneventful interactions with Kudara, Koma, and Shiragi, serious discord continued where the Soga were involved. The most serious issue was Soga no Iruka and his attempts to seize power in place of his father, Soga no Emishi. The natural disasters afflicting the people at the time were seen as a reflection of the disorder caused by these conflicts.

Soga no Emishi, who continued to serve as minister when Emperor Kōgyoku was enthroned, was a level-headed individual. However, Soga no Iruka had an aggressive personality and frequently pushed his father aside, interfering on political issues. Though he was of the highest family status, his personality was unyielding, conceited, and uncooperative. Even so, when Iruka was a boy, a scholarly priest named Min described him as a prodigy equal in talent to Nakatomi no Kamatari.[22] Though Iruka benefited from the power of the Soga, which his family had worked tirelessly to establish, he was frustrated with his father's indecisiveness and he had a strong desire to govern the state as he wished.

---

[22] See footnote 9.

One incident that pointed to Emishi's self-aggrandizement was his attempt to pray for rain in the first year of Kōgyoku (642). In the third month, *Nihon shoki* reported unusual weather patterns, stating "there were no clouds, [though] rain fell" and "this month, it [only] drizzled." In the fourth month of that year, there was an extended period of rain, in the fifth month, the crops ripened, and in the sixth month, it only drizzled. In the seventh month, there was an auspicious omen a "guest star entering the moon" (an eclipse). Furthermore, a young male servant caught a white sparrow and Emishi received another white sparrow from another person. These two events were seen as lucky omens that would help the crops. However, the drought continued. Government ministers appealed to Emishi, telling him that villagers had been conducting a Chinese "praying for rain" ritual to no effect. Emishi then ordered various temples to do sutra chanting, and, at the same time, he ordered that the Buddha statue Shitennō be placed in the south garden. Then he himself prayed for rain while burning incense. After these actions, it drizzled for a few days, but it was not enough to wet the earth. Not only had his prayers for rain failed, but his attempt was also later seen as part of the problem.

Since it had still not rained in the eigth month, Emperor Kōgyoku went to the temple Sakatadera in Minamibuchi, where he knelt down and prayed for rain in every direction while gazing up to heaven. It immediately began to thunder

Emperor Kōgyoku   *67*

and rain heavily. It rained for five days, thoroughly saturating the crops, and farmers praised the emperor's virtue. Whatever the veracity of this story, it was used to show the authority of the emperor and assert that "praying for rain" rituals should be conducted by the emperor, not by vassals. The appropriation of this power by the Soga was not taken lightly by supporters of the emperor. Kōgyoku's power to summon the rain was also seen as demonstrating the shamanic power of the emperor, who, in this case, was female.

This was not the only example of the Soga clan challenging the imperial family. In the ninth month of 642, Emperor Kōgyoku ordered the construction of a large temple and ships, and ordered that a palace be built by the twelfth month of the year. Notably, many instances of abnormal weather are recorded in the *Nihon shoki* during this time, such as earthquakes, rain, thunder, and spring-like warm weather during the winter months. In the same year, a memorial service was held for Emperor Jomei on the anniversary of his death. On this occasion, Emperor Kōgyoku moved into Oharida temporary palace. Soga no Emishi, who opposed her actions, built a tumulus for his ancestors at Katsuragi. Emishi also danced the *yatsuchi no mai* (a court dance based on Chinese customs), a privilege that was supposed to be reserved for emperors. He then composed the following poem:

68

> resolving to cross
> the broad rapids
> of the Oshi River in Yamato
> I bind my boot strings
> and gird my loins

yamato no / oshi no hirose wo / wataran to /
ayoi tazukuri / koshi zukurou mo

[NS 109]

Emishi also wrote a poem that said that he was preparing to cross the Soga River in the area of the Katsuragi Castle, which was the headquarters of the Soga clan. The underlying meaning was that he, a Soga, was praying for the support of his ancestors to help him take over the land by force. Furthermore, he also had the people build two tombs, one for Emishi, called Oomisasagi ("The Great Tomb"), and the other for Iruka, called Komisasagi ("The Small Tomb"). Moreover, he forced laborers[23] belonging to Prince Shōtoku to build the tombs. Emishi thus took full advantage of his position as a minister to demonstrate his authority to the people.

---

[23] *Bemin* 部民 were unfree peoples owned by influential families of the Yamato government from roughly the fifth to seventh centuries.

Emperor Kōgyoku   69

Kamitsumiya no Iratsume no himemiko (also known as Harukome), a daughter of Prince Shōtoku and consort to Yamashiro no Ooe, became angry, as the laborers Emishi had forced to work for him were in fact hers. She could not repress her anger at his rude behavior, so she openly proclaimed, "A minister, Soga, controls state affairs and often acts rudely. Just as there are not two suns, there are not two emperors on the earth. Why can he use the people for his own benefit?" She struggled against Emishi's intolerable behavior, but, her resistance, being an obstacle for the Soga, eventually resulted in her family being destroyed.

Soga no Iruka continued to control politics and planned to eventually destroy the family of Prince Shōtoku in order to allow Prince Furuhito to ascend to the throne. At the time Iruka attacked Sakaibe no Marise and Yamashiro no Ooe at Ikaruga no miya, Yamshiro no Ooe and his family escaped to Ikoyama, but they returned to Ikaruga no miya, where he and his family committed suicide. With this, Iruka destroyed Prince Shōtoku's line. Prince Shōtoku left a glorious legacy of achievements, but his descendants, regardless of whether or not they were involved in these political machinations, were killed. When Emishi heard about his son's disgraceful behavior, he told Iruka, "You are foolish. You are not safe from danger, either."

A supposed popular nursery rhyme of the time said the following:

a little monkey
is sitting on the big rock
roasting rice —
eat some rice yourself and be off
you old mountain goat

iwa no ue ni / kozaru kome yaku / kome danimo /
tagete toorase / yamashishi no oji

In the rhyme, "the big rock" meant the residences where
Prince Shōtoku's family lived, "a little monkey" referred to
Soga no Iruka, "roasting rice" meant to burn the palace, and
the "old mountain goat" was Yamashiro no Ooe, who ran
away to the mountain.

One person who was distressed by the despotic behavior
of the Soga was Nakatomi no Kamako (also known as
Kamatari, 614-669). Although only thirty-one years old, he
became Councilor of Divinities (*jingi no kami*)[24] and was
well-educated. Nakatomi no Kamako had a strong sense of
justice and wanted to curb Iruka's influence. He had great
faith in Prince Karu no miko (who was a younger brother of

---

[24] Also known as *jingihaku*, the *jingi no kami* 神祇伯 was an
imperial minister who acted as director of the Department of
Divinities (*jingikan*) and managed important ceremonial events.

Emperor Kōgyoku and the later Emperor Kōtoku, 596-654), and when he looked for a member of the emperor's family to lead a coup against Iruka, he looked to Karu no miko. Unfortunately, Prince Karu no miko had leg ailments and was unsuitable for the task. He looked next to Prince Naka no Ooe as a potential leader. It is a famous story that Nakatomi no Kamako played *kemari*[25] with Prince Naka no Ooe at Hōkōji Temple to become closer to the prince. After that, the two became fast friends and in secret began to plan the defeat of the Soga.

Nihon shoki describes various strange events that occurred in the days before their plan was put into action. For example, when the Soga minister crossed a bridge, a *fugeki*[26] began praying to the *kami*; elderly people who witnessed the event interpreted it as a sign of the changing times. In addition, during this period, the belief had spread that if you worshipped an insect spirit on the banks of the Fujikawa River, you would become wealthy. Consequently, many people lost their assets, and the one who resolved the resulting turmoil was Hatano Kawakatsu, a semi-legendary figure who supposedly served under a number of emperors.[27] This

---

[25] *Kemari* 蹴鞠 is an ancient ball game popular among courtiers that was similar to soccer and/or hacky sack.

[26] *Fugeki* 巫覡 were a kind of spiritual diviner (either male or female).

72

incident became a symbol of the Soga's inability to address social problems. Perhaps because of the danger perceived from these unsettling circumstances, Soga no Emishi and Iruka built new mansions next to one another in the hills of Amakashi in Asuka. They called their residences *mikado* (literally "palace gates" and a homonym for "emperor") and their children *miko* ("regal child"). Preparing for the possibility of future attacks by their enemies, they build well-fortified houses.

The day came on the twelfth day of the sixth month in 645, when Prince Naka no Ooe and Kamatari (Nakatomi no Kamako) attacked. This was the same day on which the court was to receive envoys from Kudara, Koma, and Shiragi. The emperor and cabinet ministers (including Iruka and Emishi) gathered at the Imperial Council Hall (*daigokuden*), and the ceremony began. The coup was executed by Prince Naka no Ooe and Kamatari as planned, with Naka no Ooe killing Iruka. Fleeing to his residence, Emishi set a fire which burned *Tennōki*, *Kokki*,[28] and other treasures, with only *Kokki* surviving. This incident must have been shocking for Emperor Kōgyoku to witness before the court, and may have

---

[27] For a detailed translation and explanation of this incident in the *Nihon shoki*, see Michael I. Como, *Shotoku: Ethnicity, Ritual, and Violence in the Japanese Buddhist Tradition* (Oxford and New York: Oxford University Press, 2008), 51-52.

Emperor Kōgyoku   73

been a motivation for abdicating the throne.

Prince Naka no Ooe discussed the matter of who should succeed to the throne with Kamatari, and Kamatari suggested handing over the throne to Prince Naka no Ooe's uncle, Prince Karu, instead. However, Prince Furuhito announced that he did not have any intention to ascend to become emperor, but instead wished to enter the priesthood and support the emperor in spirit from that position. This led to the enthronement of Prince Karu as Emperor Kōtoku (r. 645-654), and on the fourteenth day of the sixth month, Emperor Kōgyoku abdicated and passed the throne to her younger brother, Prince Karu, who became Emperor Kōtoku.

The *Nihon shoki* records little of Emperor Kōgyoku's achievments. Having spent roughly three-and-a-half years entangled with the Soga, her political activities are largely overshadowed by records of the Soga family intrigues.

---

[28] *Tennōki* (Record of Emperors) and *Kokki* (National Record) were two invaluable historical records of the state, some of the earliest known to be produced.

Emperor Saimei
(r. 655-661)

Translated by Masako Hamada

*The first female emperor who reascended
the throne under a new name.*

Reascension

Emperor Kōgyoku was both the second and the third female emperor. After passing the throne to her brother, Emperor Kōgyoku was given the honor title of Sumemioya no mikoto.[29] She was the first emperor to give up the throne during her lifetime and later reascend it. That in and of itself was a significant event in Japanese history. There have been only two cases of reascension, the other being that of Emperor Kōken, who returned to the throne as Emperor Shōtoku in the Nara period. Interestingly, the only two cases of reascension were both by female emperors.

---

[29] This was a temporary title of honor, given that the title "retired emperor (*daijō tennō*)" did not yet exist.

Emperor Saimei

Before her time as Emperor Kōgyoku and before becoming consort to Emperor Jomei, she was married to Prince Takamuku, grandson of Emperor Yōmei. She had a son, Prince Aya, by Prince Takamuku, but the name Takamuku cannot be found among the grandchildren of Emperor Yōmei in the royal family record. It is thought he might be the figure Takamuku no Kuromaro. Since most of the previous empresses were from the Soga clan, it is not known why Emperor Jomei selected the previously married Kōgyoku as his consort. This may have been a reflection of her compelling character, evident in her tenure as Emperor Saimei.

Circumstances Prior to Saimei's Enthronement

With the Soga subjugated, Emperor Kōgyoku abdicated the throne, but before she did, she issued an imperial edict stating that she wanted Prince Naka no Ooe to be the next emperor. However, after consulting with Kamatari, she changed her mind and recommended that her younger brother, Prince Karu, become emperor instead.

Prince Karu declined and recommended Prince Furuhito, a half-brother of Prince Naka no Ooe. However, Prince Furuhito, a blood relative of the recently defeated Soga clan, had no desire to become emperor, so he took the tonsure, becoming a monk, and secluded himself in Yoshino. As a

76

result, Prince Karu was reluctantly enthroned as the thirty-sixth emperor, Emperor Kōtoku, at the late age of fifty years old. Prince Naka no Ooe became crown prince, the position of cabinet minister (which had been dominated by the Soga) was abolished, the courtier Abe no Kurahashimaro was once again appointed as Minister of the Left (*Sadaijin*), and Soga no Yamada Ishikawamaro was appointed as Minister of the Right (*Udaijin*).[30] Kamatari was appointed as an imperial advisor, and the priest Min and Takamuku no Kuromaro, both well trusted by Emperor Kōgyoku, were appointed as ministers of education. Although Emperor Kōtoku appointed loyal figures to key roles in his new administration, this did not guarantee that his administration progressed without incident.

In the section of *Nihon shoki* on Emperor Kōtoku, it states that "[Kōtoku] respected Buddhism and made light of the way of the gods,"[31] but there are comparatively few entries on Buddhism. Furthermore, descriptions suggest that

---

[30] Two of the highest political positions assisting the emperor, the Minister of the Left and the Minister of the Right were so named because of their seating positions beside the emperor during formal events. Typically, the Minister of the Left was slightly more powerful than that of the Right.

[31] "The way of the gods" refers to ritual practices of *kami* worship for which emperors, especially, were responsible as heads of state.

Emperor Saimei 77

he had a reserved, scholarly personality and enjoyed Confucian doctrine. In Kōtoku 4 (645), Emperor Kōtoku named the era "Taika," and the *nengo* system[32] of differentiating periods of time by era names formally began. In the seventh month, he made Princess Hashihito his empress. A daughter of Emperor Kōgyoku, Hashihito was a half-sister of Prince Naka no Ooe by the same mother and also a niece of the emperor. Kōtoku also had two consorts. One of them was Otarashi, a daughter of the Minister of the Left (Abe Kurahashimaro), by whom she had a son, Prince Arima. The other was Chichi no Iratsume, a daughter of the Minster of the Right (Ishikawamaro). Emperor Kōtoku thus solidified political relationships through marriage using central figures in his new government. In the twelfth month of 645, he transferred the capital to Nagara toyosaki in Naniwa. This location was far from the previous political center of Asuka, but it was a convenient location for traveling to foreign states and to administer domestic affairs.

---

[32] *Nengo* 年号 is the Japanese system of identifying years according to the name of the era. The first of the two elements identifies the year in the Japanese era calendar scheme. The second element, a number, counts the years since the era began; as in many other systems, there is no year zero. Era names were frequently changed when something special happened, such as a new emperor's enthronement, or an extraordinary natural phenomenon occurred.

The following year, the emperor announced the famous "Imperial Decree of Reform." Now known as the "Taika Reforms," these policies initiated political changes that emulated the system of administrative and legal codes of the T'ang Dynasty in China. From 645 until Hakuchi 1 (650), these new systems of law were successively implemented. Those responsible for this major undertaking were Prince Naka no Ooe and Nakatomi no Kamatari, though it took some years to fully realize the reforms.

Other events during this period of time included the dispatching of envoys to the T'ang Dynasty and exchanges with the states of the Korean peninsula. Practitioners of Buddhism from the continent frequently traveled to Japan. Kōtoku also had the leisure time to travel to a hot spring in Ki province and visited his temporary residence at Koshiro.

After six years, the construction of Nagara toyosaki no miya was completed and the emperor took up residence there. Soon after, the Minister of the Left, Abe no Kurahashimaro, died from illness, and Soga no Himuka, a scheming half-brother of the Ishikawamaro (the Minister of the Right), saw this as an opportunity to also depose his sibling. Himuka deceived Prince Naka no Ooe, secretly informing him that Ishikawamaro was planning a rebellion against the emperor. As a result, Ishikawamaro was attacked by imperial forces and subsequently killed himself. Princess Miyatsuko (also known as Ochi no Iratsune), who was the consort of Prince

Naka no Ooe and daughter of Ishikawamaro, died of shock from this incident. Eventually, the emperor discovered that Himuka had falsified this information and Himuka was exiled to the Dazaifu in Kyushu. This altercation was troubling, but it did not greatly impact Emperor Kōtoku's reign.

The emperor and crown prince had for some time been at odds with one another over diplomatic tensions between the T'ang and the Korean kingdoms, and, in the fall of Hakuchi 4 (654), Crown Prince Naka no Ooe led his family to withdraw from the palace at Naniwa and move to a residence in Asuka. He was joined by the retired emperor, Kōgyoku, and Empress Hashihito. Feeling forlorn and resentful at their seeming betrayal, the Emperor Kōtoku sent a poem to the empress who had abandoned him:

> the tethered mount
> I reared and tended,
> never letting loose,
> will anybody find
> that horse I care for?

kanaki tsuke / a ga kau koma wa / hikidesezu /
a ga kau koma o / hito mitsuran ka

[NS 118]

In this poem, the horse is used as a metaphor for the empress. The *Nihon shoki* also recorded that when Naka no Ooe, the empress, and others moved from the capital, even the rats fled from Naniwa (though this may only be polemical commentary).

In the fall of Hakuchi 5 (655), Emperor Kōtoku became ill at the Toyosaki no miya in Naniwa. The empress, crown prince, Retired Emperor Kōgyoku, and all the court officials came to see him, but he died shortly thereafter. Prince Naka no Ooe requested that his mother, Retired Emperor Kōgyoku (known then as Sumemioya no mikoto) move to a temporary residence in Kawabe, paving the way for Kōgyoku to return to the throne and become Emperor Saimei.

The Enthronement of Emperor Saimei

Nihon shoki does not discuss the reason why Kōgyoku, a former emperor, was enthroned again instead of Crown Prince Naka no Ooe after Emperor Kōtoku's passing. While this invites speculation, the reason may have been obvious to people at the time. One possibility is the crown prince's relationship with Empress Hashihito, which was rumored to be incestuous. As long as there was a possibility of an improper relationship, he could not be enthroned. Publicly, Naka no Ooe reasoned that his position as crown prince gave him more political freedom than being emperor, and so he

Emperor Saimei   *81*

gave up on any ambitions for the throne. Furthermore, he also
did not want Prince Arima, Emperor Kōtoku's son, to ascend.
The solution was thus for his mother to take the throne a
second time. Emperor Kōgyoku's second accession was the
first such occurence in Japan.

It is unclear why Emperor Kōgyoku readily agreed to
take the throne as Emperor Saimei. She may have received
advice from Kamatari, although other close advisors such as
Min and Takamuku no Kuromaro were already dead. If she
herself took the throne, her beloved son would be next in line
to become emperor, and she may not have wanted to
relinquish the imperial throne to other members of the royal
family. In this sense, Emperor Saimei may have served as an
intermediary emperor. She was sixty-two years old and one of
the oldest emperors enthroned in Japanese history. Her
accession took place in Saimei 1 (655) at Asuka Itabuki
Palace.

The Continuous Construction Projects of Emperor Saimei

Asuka Itabuki Palace (literally, "Asuka shingle-roofed
palace") was given its name when the previous miscanthus
reed-thatched roofs were replaced by cypress bark shingle
roofs. In the winter of that year (655), this building was
destroyed in a fire, and Emperor Saimei ordered the
construction of a new palace roofed with ceramic tiles in

Oharida. While it was being built, she lived in the Asuka Kawara no miya. However, the construction work encountered many difficulties and the plan to build the new structure was abandoned. Nevertheless, the emperor built another residence in Asuka Okamoto, in the following year. It is difficult to tell whether Emperor Saimei simply had an affinity for building, or if the people close to the emperor wanted to show their emperor's prestige to the imperial court and the public. The new location, Asuka Okamoto, was the location of her late husband Emperor Jomei's residence, making it dear to her. She named the palace, "The Latter Okamoto Residence." She then ordered that the Tamu no mine hill (now called Tōno mine) to the east of Asuka be enclosed with fences. A watchtower (*takadono*, literally "tall manor") was built on the top of the hill beside two zelkova trees, and so the residence was called Futatsuki no miya ("double zelkova residence") or sometimes Amatsu no miya ("heavenly residence").

Watchtowers were, as their name suggests, tall structures, and originally the term was used for Taoist temples in China. Because of this, some scholars speculate that Emperor Saimei may have been interested in Taoism, which had been introduced and practiced privately in Japan during that time. Furthermore, a long ditch was dug between the west side of Ama no Kaguyama and Isonokami no Yama, forming a canal lined with rocks allowing water to flow through the

Emperor Saimei

area. A large tortoise-shaped stone structure was also uncovered in recent excavations. Although their purpose is unknown, there is a possibility that the emperor was emulating models from China or Kudara. She may also have been influenced by Taoist architecture or even Zoroastrianism from Persia.

Regardless of the reasons behind these projects, such large-scale undertakings put a heavy burden on the people. Of the dissatisfaction of the people, one record stated, "The [emperor's] canal was foolish. It required tremendous resources, taking as many as 30,000 laborers to plan and 70,000 to build the walls. [Meanwhile] the timbers of the palace have festered and the top of the mountain collapsed." In spite of the public outcry, she built a residence in Yoshino even though there was already an imperial villa there. Emperor Suiko had visited this villa and Emperor Saimei had used it during her reign as Emperor Kōgyoku to hold the *toyo no akari no sechi e* court banquet.[33] Saimei's construction of a new villa in Yoshino may have actually been a reconstruction of a very old building. Two years later, in the third month of 659, she once again held the *toyo no akari no sachie* there,

---

[33] The *toyo no akari no sechi e* 豊明節会 is a banquet held following the annual festival of offering the first rice harvest to the gods (*shinjōsai*).

84

although it is unclear why she chose to hold it in the spring instead of its usual time in the fall along with the First Offering Harvest Rites (*daijōsai*) following enthronement.[34] Soon after the Yoshino villa was completed, the latter Okamoto residence was destroyed by fire.

The emperor's enthusiasm for construction and engineering continued. Saimei had imitations of Mt. Sumeru (a sacred imaginary mountain in Buddhist cosmology) constructed, one built to the west of Asukaji Temple in the seventh month of the third year and another to the east of Amakashi no Oka in the third month of the fifth year.[35] Then, she invited representatives of Tokara (possibly a kingdom situated in the area of present-day Thailand) and Ezo (northern Japan) to visit there, where she held banquets. This emphasis on Buddhist ideology did not mean that Emperor Saimei disregarded Shinto practice. In the seventh month of that year, she constructed the Grand Shrine of Kumano in Izumo, and in the seventh year she traveled to the Tachibana

---

[34] *Shinjosai* 新嘗祭 is a royal ritual for the harvest of rice held every year in the fall. The emperor makes an offering of the first crop of rice to the gods, and the emperor eats the new rice. *Daijosai* 大嘗祭 is the first *shinjosai* for the newly enthroned emperor.

[35] Saimei also constructed one more Mt. Sumeru imitation, near Ishinokami pond. Torquil Duthie, *Man'yōshū and the Imperial Imagination in Early Japan* (Leiden: Brill, 2014), 96.

Emperor Saimei 85

no Hironiwa residence in Asakura to build a villa. However, the latter plan was discarded, because the builders felled sacred trees for the project and had seemingly incurred the deity's displeasure. Nevertheless, Saimei became known for her various architectural endeavors.

On the other hand, Emperor Saimei's legacy also included tragic personal affairs. In the fifth month of the fourth year of her reign (658), Emperor Saimei's beloved grandson, Prince Takeru, died at the age of eight. Born of her son, Prince Naka no Ooe and Ochi no Iratsume, Prince Takeru was unable to speak from birth, which made him very dear to them. Saimei was heartbroken by his death, and she instructed the officials to move his remains after she died to the mausoleum she was to be buried in. After Takeru's death, Saimei composed the following poem:

> as there is no break
> in the flow of flooding water
> of the Asuka River,
> so there is no end at all
> to my yearning for him

asukagawa / minagirai tsutsu / iku mizu no /
aida mo naku mo / omo'oyuru kamo

[NS 121]

Reflecting her mournful feelings for her late grandson, Saimei's emotions continued to ceaselessly "flow." In autumn of the same year, Emperor Saimei went to a hot spring at Muro in Kii province. The following is one of the poems she composed there:

> even if I cross mountains,
> or traverse the seas,
> will I ever be able to forget
> his pale white face
> off in snow-bound Imaki?

yama koete / umi wataru tomo / omoshiroki /
imaki no uchi wa / wasurayu mashiji

[NS 122]

Imaki is a place where Emperor Saimei spent time with Prince Takeru as well as the place he was buried.

There are five poems in the first volume of the *Man'yōshū* that include the name "Naka no Sumera mikoto" said to be composed by Empress Hashihito, but they may also have been written by Emperor Saimei.[36]

---

[36] MYS 1.3, 1.4, 1.10, 1.11, and 1.12.

The Prince Arima Incident

The Prince Arima Incident also occurred during the reign of Emperor Saimei. Prince Arima was a son of Emperor Kōtoku and Otarashi hime. When his father died, he was one of the candidates to succeed him, but Prince Naka no Ooe was the most likely to be chosen. Emperor Kōtoku was also expected to be an intermediary emperor, as the line was originally offered to Prince Naka no Ooe. In the end, however, Naka no Ooe declined and the former emperor Kōgyoku reascended as Emperor Saimei. With his hopes for ascending the throne dashed, Prince Arima began to behave as if mentally disturbed, though it is uncertain whether or not this was truly mental fatigue or just a ploy. He traveled to the Muro hot spring in Kii province, purportedly for recuperation, and recovered.

Hearing of her nephew's recovery, Emperor Saimei made an imperial visit to Muro, accompanied by her family and many officials, leaving the capital understaffed. This was a golden opportunity for Prince Arima, and, given the absence of the court, Soga no Akae (a prominent member of the Soga family) took advantage of the moment to make false accusations against the emperor to Arima and foment rebellion. He claimed that the emperor had committed three crimes. First, she had built many storehouses and was amassing a fortune from what she took from the people, who

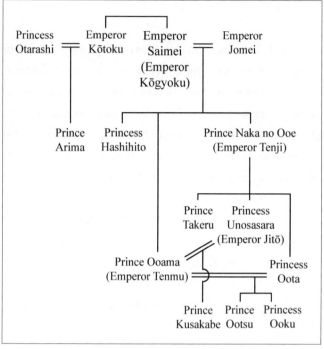

Lineage of Emperor Saimei

suffered heavy taxes. Second, she had wasted significant revenues on the construction of long canals. Third, she had built "mountains" by transporting a large number of rocks by boat.[37]

With this information, Prince Arima felt that his time had finally come, and, with rebellion in mind, he held a secret meeting at the watchtower of Akae's residence. However, during the meeting, the prince's armrest broke, and the

Emperor Saimei

89

discussion was cut short, with Arima returning home. In the middle of the night, Akae had palace laborers surround the prince's residence and quickly sent word to the emperor at Muro to inform her of Arima's plot.

Prince Arima had been wholly deceived. It may have been because the person who was in charge in the emperor's absence had the emperor's confidence, or, it may have been a plot by Prince Naka no Ooe, who foresaw Prince Arima's rebellion. Whatever the case, Prince Arima was arrested and escorted to the emperor at Muro. During the long journey to Kii province, he wrote the following poem, which was recorded in *Man'yōshū*:

> If I pluck and bind
> some branches from
> Iwashiro's pine woods beach,
> good fortune may take me back
> to gaze upon it once again

iwashiro no / hama matsu ga e o / hiki musubi /

---

[37] This apparently was done in connection to the perceived need to take defensive measures against a possible Korean invasion. For more information, see D. M. Brown, *The Cambridge History of Japan, Vol. 1, Ancient Japan* (Cambridge: Cambridge University Press, 1993), 201-210.

masakiku araba / mata kaeri min

were I at home, my food
would be served in a fine bowl;
when travelling, with
grass for my pillow, food is
piled on an oaktree leaf

ie ni areba / ke ni moru ii o / kusamakura /
tabi ni shi areba / shii no ha ni moru

[MYS 2.141-142]

Binding branches of pine and praying for his own safety, Prince Arima offered rice to the deities, praying for good fortune while on distant travel, and when he was asked by Crown Prince Naka no Ooe about the rebellious plot, Arima answered, "Heaven and Akae should know. I do not." Though his composition "good fortune may take me back" suggests he held onto a sliver of hope, on the way back to the capital, Prince Arima was executed by strangulation at Fujishiro no Saka. He would never see those bound pine branches again. Arima was nineteen years old at the time. Although his execution was not a rare occurrence in that era, many people felt compassion for Prince Arima. Within a short amount of time, Prince Arima's story was seen as sympathetic. The second poem (above) was composed by

Yamanoue no Okura, who felt deep deeply for the prince and his misfortune. While Prince Naka no Ooe was at the center of this affair, Emperor Saimei may have also been involved from its outset.

Sending Reinforcements to Kudara

Another prominent aspect of Emperor Saimei's reign was diplomatic realtions with the Emishi and the peoples on the Korean peninsula.[38] Already during her time as Emperor Kōgyoku, Saimei had entertained emissaries of the Emishi at court, and, as a part of the Taika Reforms, two fortresses were built in Nutari and Iwafune to maintain security at the edges of Emishi territory. Abe no Hirafu also engaged in two campaigns against the Emishi between 658 and 660, encountering opposition from another ethnic group, the Michihase (who may have been Ainu).

Meanwhile, the Shiragi kingdom had allied with the T'ang dynasty and was attacking Kudara. Kishitsu Fukushin, a general from Kudara, who had for some time maintained friendly relations with the Japanese court, asked Saimei for reinforcements. However, the court was divided on this

---

[38] The Emishi were an ethnic group of peoples who occupied northeastern Honshu.

matter; although it had good relations with Kudara, the court also had envoys dispatched to the T'ang and Japanese territories in Mimana on the peninsula. The only two options were to make an enemy of the T'ang or relinquish their ties to Kudara. Emperor Saimei struggled with the decision, but, in the end, she decided to send reinforcements to Kudara. She traveled to the Naniwa Palace and from there departed for Tsukushi, ordering for troops to be dispatched. It was a serious state affair.

On the sixth day of the first month of Saimei 7 (661), a fleet of vessels carrying Emperor Saimei, Prince Naka no Ooe, Prince Ooama, and various high officials of the court left the port of Naniwa for Chikushi. On the ninth day, during a stop at Ooku in Kibi, Princess Oota, a consort of Prince Ooama, gave birth to a baby girl. They gave her the name of her birthplace, calling her Princess Ooku.[39] Although it would normally be unthinkable for a woman to take on such long travel in the final term of her pregnancy, and this seems like a trifling detail to record, it may have been included in the *Nihon shoki* because of its connection to Prince Ootsu (663-686) and Prince Naka no Ooe. As for Saimei, Ooku was her

---

[39] Princess Ooku was not only a daughter of Naka no Ooe and the older sister of the later Emperor Jitō (r. 686-697), but Ooku also later gave birth to Prince Ootsu.

Emperor Saimei 93

granddaughter. The later Emperor Jitō, known then as Princess Unosasara, was also a consort of Prince Ooama at that time, and would later give birth to Prince Kusakabe.

The imperial ship anchored at the harbor of Nigita in Iyo province (today, Shikoku) on the fourteenth day, and the emperor and her party stayed at a temporary imperial residence known as Iwayu, which is thought to be the present-day Dōgo hot spring. Princess Nukada, who was travelling with them, composed the following poem:

> setting forth
> by boat from Nigitatsu
> after waiting for the moon,
> the tide is with us,
> let us row our way forth

nigitatsu ni / funanori sento / tsuki mateba /
shio mo kanainu / ima wa kogi idena

[MYS 1.8]

The imperial ship arrived at the port of Ootsu at Na (modern day Hakata) in the third month. In the fifth month, the emperor left the ship and took up residence in Asakura Tachibana no Hironiwa in Hakata. According to the *Nihon shoki*, the deities still bore a grudge against the emperor for felling the sacred trees of Asakura shrine and destroyed the building. The emperor grew ill, perhaps because of the stress of her travels. She died there two months later at the age of sixty-eight. It had been six years since her enthronement. The *Nihon shoki* also claims a large ogre was seen looking down from atop a mountain on the funeral of Saimei when she passed away and had also done so at her coronation. Many mysterious phenomena and figures such as this appear in stories surrounding Emperor Saimei. Crown Prince Naka no Ooe wrote the following poem, thinking of his mother:

> because I so dearly
> love your eyes,
> I weighed anchor here,
> and loving so deeply
> I yearn for the sight of you

kimi ga me no / koishiki karani / hatete ite /
kakuya koimumo / kimi ga me o hori

[NS 126]

The emperor's body was brought to Naniwa and then solemnly returned to the temporary residence at Asuka kawaberi.

In the historical record, Saimei's time as Emperor Kōgyoku was overshadowed by the politics of the Soga family. However, as Emperor Saimei, she was a visible and dynamic ruler. Although the one who took the helm of politics was Crown Prince Naka no Ooe, as Emperor Saimei, she was a presence of great importance. Though in her sixties, she was active and dignified, overcoming the image of a mere "intermediary" emperor.

After Emperor Saimei's death, Naka no Ooe did not immediately ascend to the throne, but continued to be in command of the reinforcement army for Kudara. In the end, however, in 663 Kudara and Prince Naka no Ooe's army were defeated by a Shiragi and T'ang allied army at Hakusuki no e.

Emperor Jitō
(r. 686-697)

Translated by Masako Iino

A central figure of the imperial court by birth.
A familiar figure in the Ogura hyakunin isshu
seen as a capable emperor.

Emperor Jitō was the fourth female emperor. Jitō is recognized for her brilliance and her presence. Today, if someone is asked to give the name of a female emperor, they would most likely say Emperor Jitō. She was an emperor during a period of great change in Japan's history, and also frequently appears in important poetic collections, such as the *Man'yōshū* and *Hyakunin isshu*.

The first two female emperors, Emperors Suiko and Kōgyoku/Saimei, emerged from somewhat unremarkable lineages, being related or wed to lesser-known fathers and husbands. The first female emperor, Emperor Suiko, was the daughter of Emperor Kinmei and became the empress of Emperor Bidatsu. Emperor Kinmei may be a familiar name to some, but not many recognize Bidatsu. The second (or third) female emperor, Emperor Kōgyoku/Saimei, was a daughter of

Prince Chinu, who was grandson of Emperor Bidatsu. Kōgyoku's husband, Emperor Jomei, was son of Prince Oshisaka Hikoto, who was son of Bidatsu. These women were chosen to be emperors in order to preserve the imperial blood line, rather than for their distinguished familial connections. They are therefore commonly evaluated according to their capabilities as sovereigns.

In the case of Emperor Jitō, she was not only a central figure of the imperial family by birth, but also a forceful personality. She was born the daughter of Prince Naka no Ooe, who solidified the political footing of the Yamato imperial court's reign by overthrowing the powerful Soga clan to become Emperor Tenji. She was also closely involved in government affairs as the empress of Emperor Tenmu, Emperor Tenji's brother. Emperor Tenmu was both a strong supporter of Emperor Tenji as well as one of the figures responsible for laying the groundwork for the *ritsuryō* state system.[40] With such a background, Emperor Jitō demonstrated a power and ingenuity not seen in the previous two female emperors. She furthermore had a charisma that the emperors who followed her lacked. Before going into

---

[40] The legal system modeled on China that was codified by the ancient court was generally called *ritsuryō* 律令, *ritsu* referring to penal codes and *ryō* to administrative codes.

98

the period of Emperor Jitō's reign, we will first touch upon the reigns of Emperor Tenji and Emperor Tenmu, both of which Jitō observed firsthand and in which she herself was involved.

Emperor Tenji

The previous Emperor Saimei died suddenly while traveling to conquer Tsukushi. Prince Naka no Ooe, who wielded political power at the time, continued to handle political affairs as crown prince without succeeding to the throne. This was a rare occurrence, known in Japan as *shōsei*, in which the person next in line for the throne declines to ascend to it. One reason for this unusual situation may have been the unnaturally close relationship between Naka no Ooe and his sister, Princess Hashihito. Prince Naka no Ooe was officially enthroned as emperor three years after Hashihito passed away, and by then he had been crown prince for twenty-three years. Naka no Ooe now began to handle political affairs as emperor in a way quite different than when he was crown prince under Emperor Saimei. At the time, he also needed to establish a united front with his younger brother, Prince Ooama. He may have occasionally taken a step back from the spotlight and put his brother forward in order to strengthen internal affairs of the court. In 664, three decrees were issued: the reform of the court rank system,

Emperor Jitō   99

establishment of a clan system, and the revival of the *bemin* system of occupational groups in service to the court.[41] These decrees were intended to revitalize local influential clans and to formulate a centralized state with a powerful emperor as its core. Under this state system, a primary concern was having defenses against foreign enemies, and therefore, the administration also stipulated the establishment of guards (*sakimori*) and moated fortresses (*mizuki*).

Sakimori were a kind of security force stationed in strategic locations of interaction with the continent, such as Tsushima, Iki, and Tsukushi. They were typically made up of farmers from the northeastern provinces appointed to *sakimori* positions. Traveling to these distant locations was a great burden for those living in the east. These difficulties are expressed in a number of poems composed by *sakimori* and their families. These poems were compiled in the *Man'yōshū* by the courtier Ootomo no Yakamochi (c. 718-785). Yakamochi held a position in the Ministry of Military Affairs, the office responsible for *sakimori*; the voices of *sakimori* poets are thus preserved through his efforts. The following poems are among them:

---

[41] See footnote 23.

by the rocky shores
I cross the broad seas
to serve my great lord
leaving behind
my father and mother

ookimi no / mikoto kashikomi / iso ni furi /
unabara wataru / chichi haha okite

[MYS 20.4328]

when I stand on the slope
of Mount Ashigara
and wave my sleeve,
will my beloved at home
see me clearly ?

ashigara no / misaka ni tashite / sode furaba /
iwa naru imo wa / saya ni mimo kamo

[MYS 20.4423]

when I see someone asking,
as the border guard sets off,
whose husband is he ?
I wish I were she who is
without a worried heart

Emperor Jitō   *101*

sakimori ni / yuku wa ta ga se to / tou hito o /
miru ga tomoshi sa / mono omoi mo sezu

[MYS 20.4425]

These poems articulate the candid feelings of the *sakimori* assigned to protect their country.

Along with the appointment of *sakimori*, *mizuki* were established in the area around Dazaifu for defensive purposes. The *Nihon shoki* states "A large-scale embankment was built to store water. It was called *mizuki*." Mountain fortresses were also built in Dazaifu, Iki, and Tsushima, and even at the border of Yamato and Kawachi provinces in preparation for a possible invasion of foreign enemies, though no invasion ever occurred.

In 665, Princess Hashihito passed away and, in the spring of 667, when the funerary rites were completed, Prince Naka no Ooe suddenly moved the capital to Ootsu in Ōmi province. Ōmi was not in the Kinai area, where the capital had been previously located.[42] The court was suspicious of the move, and begrudged the material and emotional stress caused by the transition. As was often the case, many popular songs satirized the relocation and a certain amount of

---

[42] Kinai refers to five local provinces under the direct control of the court: Settsu, Kawachi, Izumi, Yamato, and Yamashiro.

social disorder followed. Having moved the capital from Yamato to the distant Ōmi without consulting the people, Prince Naka no Ooe most likely made this decision with defense against domestic enemies in mind. Ootsu, being on Lake Biwa, was a key location for access to the eastern provinces as well as the Hokuriku area and provinces to the west. For the purpose of unifying the provinces, Ootsu was more favorably located than Yamato and Nanba. Kakinomoto no Hitomaro, a court poet at the time, composed a *chōka* (long poem) on the move of the court to Ōmi. In it, he questions, "What was the Prince's wish?" The Prince clearly had a certain "wish" to move the capital. Moreover, people in premodern Japan had a strong consciousness of death as a polluting force, and there was a tradition that the capital was moved upon the death of an emperor and the enthronement of a new one, so one theory follows that the move of the capital occurred in response to the death of Empress Dowager Hashihito, despite the fact she was not emperor. There was, however, no known direct connection between this motivation to move the capital and the location of Ōmi.

When a capital was moved, it was common for the entirety of the court, including those in military and civil positions, to follow suit. Their homes, too, were transferred to the new site. The relocation of the capital was, conceptually, as much a move of a political location as it was a movement of those who occupied that space. As the court members proceeded from their homes in Asuka to Ōmi to their right, they could see Mt. Miwa. A calm and peaceful location, Mt. Miwa had been considered to be a *kami* since ancient times. Princess Nukada, who was accompanying Naka no Ooe during the move, is said to have gazed upon the mountain until it was too far off to be seen, and wrote a poem as follows:

> do you hide
> Mount Miwa in this way?
> at least you clouds should
> have a heart and not
> conceal it like this

miwayama o / shikamo kakusu ka / kumo danimo / kokoro aranamo / kakusō beshi ya

[MYS 1.18]

A talented poet, many of Nukada's poems are included in the *Man'yōshū*, and her exchange of poems with Prince Ooama (the future Emperor Tenmu) at Shino is particularly well known. As Tenmu's consort, Nukada gave birth to Princess To'ochi. It is theorized that some time later she may have been summoned to become Emperor Tenji's consort as well. Nukada made her story immortal with her poem comparing her own love triangle with Emperor Tenmu and Emperor Tenji to the three mountains in Yamato; according to legend, Mt. Miminashi and Mt. Ama no kagu quarreled for the favor of Mt. Unebi. Being of high birth, Princess Nukada also played a role in conducting Shinto rituals at the court. She may have composed her poem about Mt. Miwa not on the road to Ōmi, but while conducting rituals to pray for safe travel to Mt. Miwa, where the *kami* Oomono nushi no mikoto is enshrined.

In the first month of 668, Prince Naka no Ooe was finally enthroned as Emperor Tenji at Ootsu Shrine in Ōmi. Seven years had passed since the Naka no Ooe's *shōsei* rulership had begun. At the time of accession, Princess Yamato was also appointed his empress. Yamato was the daughter of his half-brother, Prince Furuhito. Emperor Tenji did not have a child from his marriage with Princess Yamato, but maintained four consorts of third-rank status, known as *hin*. One such consort was Ochi no Iratsume, daughter of Soga no Ishikawamaro, who bore Tenji three children, Princess Oota, Princess Uno, and Prince Takeru. Prince Takeru, who was the first in line to succeed the emperor, died of disease at the age of eight. It was an incident that deeply saddened his father and his grandmother, Emperor Saimei. The second daughter, Princess Uno, would later become Emperor Jitō. The emperor had fourteen children in all. Princess Oota was the mother of Princess Ooku and Prince Ootsu. Emperor Tenji's other consorts of the *hin* rank did not have children. Among the four consorts with ranks lower than *hin*, one was the mother of Prince Kawashima, and another was the mother of Prince Ootomo. In addition to these children, there was also one more prince and six princesses. With so many children by women of different political factions of the court, the emperor was in an uneasy position regarding succcession. Furthermore, Nakatomi no Kamatari, who had served as an advisor to the emperor, passed away from illness only a year after Emperor Tenji's enthronement.

The Jinshin War

On the surface, the politics of the Ōmi court appeared to proceed without quarrel. Emperor Tenji was aided by his brother, Prince Ooama, whose status as First Minister of the Great Council of State (*daijōdaijin*) was similar to that of crown prince. Together, they established a household registry in 670 known as the *Kōgo nenjaku* and the Ōmi Codes, a twenty-two-volume set of administrative ordinances that does not survive today. Also, during this period *kanshi* (Chinese poetry) and *waka* (Japanese poetry) flourished as elegant pastimes. Yet, the emperor did not feel at ease. Already at the time of his enthronement, there had been an incident that foretold of conflict to come. Although in 664 Tenji determined that his brother Ooama would be his successor, four years later, just before his brother's enthronement he had a change of heart and decided upon his favored son, Prince Ootomo. During a court banquet in 668 hosted by the emperor at the Ootsu palace, Prince Ooama abruptly plunged his long spear into the floor. It is written in the *Taishokkan-den* (Kamatari's biography) that the emperor, shocked by Ooama's outburst, tried to capture and kill him, but Kamatari interceded and the matter was settled. Even so, both the distrust felt by the emperor and Prince Ooama's smoldering sense of dissatisfaction reached a point of no return before long. While Emperor Tenji now desired that his second son, Prince Ootomo would succeed him, his mother, a lower court lady named Uneme from Iga province, was too low-ranking to qualify as mother of an emperor. At the same time, it was not unusual for the throne to pass from older brother to younger brother, and Prince Ooama, having served as crown prince, was already qualified to be the next emperor. There was also no question that Ooama was of appropriate standing by birth, as his mother was Emperor Saimei. Adding to Emperor Tenji's conflict was the fact that Prince Ooama had two distinguished children, Prince Kusakabe and Prince Ootsu; once the throne went to Prince Ooama, there was little possibility of it returning to Tenji's family. The emperor's anguish deepened. By then, Prince Ootomo had grown to be a young man, twenty years old and highly gifted, showing outstanding ability in poetry and prose.

Emperor Jitō

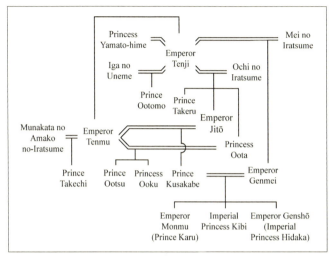

Lineage of Emperor Jitō

In 671, the emperor appointed Prince Ootomo as First Minister of the Great Council of State, thus, in effect, establishing a political system with Prince Ootomo as its core with the intention that he would succeed Tenji. Although this was an official inauguration, Prince Ooama was excluded from the process. Though the emperor surely felt anxious over the smoldering personal and political tensions at hand, time continued to pass without a confrontation. In the eighth month of that year, Emperor Tenji fell ill and it did not appear that he would recover. Finally, the emperor summoned Prince Ooama to his bedside and conveyed his wish to pass the throne to Ooama. Hiding his excitement at the unexpected words,

Ooama informed the emperor that he was actually going to become a priest, and that the empress should be enthroned as emperor and political affairs should be handled by Prince Otomo. Ooama promptly took the tonsure in the palace Buddha Hall and headed to Yoshino. In the twelfth month, Emperor Tenji's tumultuous life ended.

Although the two brothers, Emperor Tenji and Prince Ooama, both supported their mother, Emperor Saimei, through their involvement in affairs of state, this did not mean that they truly trusted one another. The tactics they employed at the emperor's deathbed, Emperor Tenji's sudden decision to once again change his mind about succession, and Ooama's unexpected decision to take the tonsure instead of accepting the throne, demonstrated that both were highly suspicious of each other. Some popular poems in *Nihon shoki* predicted the possible social unrest that death of the emperor might cause:

> Lovely Yoshino!
> the sweet fish of Yoshino
> oh yes the sweet fish
> are fine near the island
>> oh what suffering,
>> they are not distressed
>> under the water mallow
>> under the water parsley
>> oh how I am suffering!

Emperor Jitō   109

miyoshino no / yoshino no ayu / ayu koso wa /
        shima e mo yoki / e kurushi e /
nagi no moto / seri no moto / ware wa kurushi e
                                    [NS 129]

        when I, his servant,
        have not yet untied
        a single string of the eight-fold sash,
        my young lord
        has undone them all

omi no ko no / yae no himo toku / hitoe dani /
        imada tokaneba / miko no himo toku
                                    [NS 130]

        the roan-colored colt
        holds back from crossing
        through the field of arrowroot —
        some message directly given
        might be better!

akagoma no / iyuki habakaru / makuzu ga hara /
        nan no tsutekoto/tadani shi yokemu
                                    [NS 131]

110

The first poem sympathizes with the emperor's feelings by saying that although the fish are at ease, the author is full of suffering. The second poem describes a situation in which a subordinate of Prince Ooama, about to prepare himself for battle, finds that his lord is already prepared. The third suggests that both groups in Yoshino and Omi should negotiate by communicating with one another directly.

Prince Ooma brought the long-standing succession rivalry to a close in what came to be known as the Jinshin War of 672. Although Ootomo ascended to the throne, after only a few months, Ooama raised an army in Yoshino and led an attack on the troops in Ōmi, resulting in a sweeping victory. Princess Uno, Ooama's consort and the later Emperor Jitō, accompanied him during the war and eventually became a key advisor to the prince. Prince Ootomo retreated to the mountains in defeat and there ended his life. He was twenty-five years old. With this, the reign in Ōmi came to an end. Prince Ootomo's enthronement was first recorded as legitimate during the Tokugawa period (1603-1868) in *A Great History of Japan* (*Dai Nihonshi*) by Mitsukuni Tokugawa. In the Meiji period (1868-1912), he was given a posthumous title, Emperor Kōbun, and was recorded as the 39th emperor.

Emperor Tenmu

After the Jinshin War, Prince Ooama returned to Asuka and built a new palace in Asuka Kiyomigahara, where he was enthroned and became Emperor Tenmu. It is thought that the expression frequently seen in the *Man'yōshū*, "Our great sovereign is a *kami* indeed..." came into use during this period. In his imperial orders, the emperor used the term "*Kami* Incarnate (*aramikami*) and Emperor Reigning over the Eight Great Islands (*ooyashimashiyasu yamato neko sumera mikoto*)" to refer to himself. Emperor Tenmu fathered many princes and princesses: Prince Kusakabe, whose mother was Empress Uno; Princess Ooku and Prince Ootsu, whose mother was Princess Oota (the older sister of the Empress); Prince Naga and Prince Yuge, whose mother was Princess Ooe; and Prince Toneri, whose mother was Princess Niitabe. The four mothers of these princes and princesses were all daughters of Emperor Tenji, Tenmu's older brother. Marriages between close relatives were used strategically to maintain the stability of an emperor's power and influence. In addition to those children listed above, Tenmu also sired Prince Tajima with Higami no Iratsume (daughter of Kamatari); Prince Niitabe, with Ioye no Iratsume; and also Prince Hozumi, Prince Takechi, Prince Oshikabe, Prince Shiki, Princess Kino, Princess Tagata, Princess To'ochi, Princess Hatsusebe, and Princess Taki. In all, Tenmu fathered ten princes and seven princesses, and all these names are found in the *Man'yōshū*. Although being blessed with so many children meant that the emperor was able to establish a government system with his close kin at its core, it also meant that fierce quarrels among his children over imperial succession were likely imminent. Empress Uno Sasara, who was later to become Emperor Jitō, was a central figure in such struggles.

During Emperor Tenmu's reign, he actively pursued means to reinforce centralized administration under the *ritsuryō* system, such as promulgating the Asuka Kiyomihara Codes (legal codes promulgated in 689), compiling national histories, and reforming the *kabane* rank system by introducing four new titles.[43] One particularly prominent part of Tenmu's political administration was his enthusiastic religious policies. First was his support of Buddhism. Perhaps because he had previously taken the tonsure, Emperor Tenmu acted rather proactively toward Buddhism, and in the year when he was enthroned, he hand-copied the *Issai-kyō* sutra collection at Kawaharaji Temple. He then launched the construction of official temples, established Takechi Daiji Temple (later known as Daikan Daiji Temple) and Yakushiji

---

[43] *Kabane* 姓 were titles given to influential court families to denote their rank and therefore closeness to the throne.

Emperor Jitō   *113*

Temple, and also provided sustenance household grants (*jikifu*) for Kawaharaji Temple and Asukaji Temple.[44] Furthermore, Tenmu enacted sutra-copying practices and established the position of *sōgō*, priests who managed Buddhist monks and nuns. Yakushiji Temple was also founded with the specific purpose of praying for Empress Jitō to recover from illness. In 685, an imperial proclamation was issued that stated "In all the provinces there should be a Buddhist shrine in every household and thus a Buddhist statue and Buddhist scriptures will be placed there and worship performed." This proclamation became the impetus for the establishment of later provincial temples in various locations. In the portion of the *Nihon shoki* on Emperor Tenmu, there are considerably detailed sections related to Buddhism, demonstrating not simply an increased interest in Buddhism, but Tenmu's strategic political efforts to establish a system of state-controlled religion.

Entries on Shinto are even more detailed than those on Buddhism. One such example is Emperor Tenmu's reverence for Ise Shrine. It is during this time period that Ise Shrine

---

[44] *Jikifu* 食封, or sustenance household grants, were a kind of income granted to royalty and high-ranked nobles based on tax payments from specific households. *Shikifu* 職封 were awarded based on office, but similar salaries could be conferred due to rank or meritorious service.

appears explicitly in the *Kojiki* and *Nihon shoki* as the location in which the emperor's divine ancestor, the sun goddess Amaterasu, is enshrined. That Emperor Tenmu appointed his own daughter, Princess Ooku, to serve as high priestess at Ise Shrine, a position that had not been filled in fifty years, demonstrates how much importance Emperor Tenmu attached to the worship of *kami* at Ise Shrine. Ise province was also highly valued as a buffer between the capital and provinces to the east. The well-known tradition of rebuilding the main hall of the shrine every twenty years (a process known as *shikinen sengū*) is also said to have begun during this period. The emperor embraced many other regular rituals of worship aside from those at Ise Shrine. Beginning in 676, ceremonies were performed in the fourth and seventh month of every year for the *kami* of wind at Tatsuta Shrine in Yamato and the *kami* of harvest, Ooimi no kami, in Hirose. Assistance was also offered to various other shrines through occasional restorations and prayers performed. While these policies were in part a result of the emperor's personal devotion, it is also thought that he aimed to appeal to the people by enthusiastically supporting the worship of local *kami*. As the "Great Sovereign" revered as a *kami* himself, Tenmu was a man who venerated the spiritual.

Although Emperor Tenmu had gained the title of emperor, he did not choose his crown prince immediately

Emperor Jitō   *115*

after his enthronement. With so many children, and the majority of them born by different mothers, Tenmu probably spent many sleepless nights worrying over who should succeed him. Prince Kusakabe (662-689), who was born of Empress Uno Sasara (Jitō), was a sensitive child, while Prince Ootsu, born of Princess Oota, the older sister of the empress, was superior to Prince Kusakabe in all respects. Prince Kusakabe was one year older than Prince Ootsu, and both outranked the other princes, making these two the leading candidates for crown prince. In the fifth month of Tenmu 8 (680) the emperor, having been unable to decide, took the empress and six of the princes, Kusakabe, Ootsu, Takechi, Oshikabe, Kawashima, and Shiki, to the Yoshino Palace. The last two were Emperor Tenji's children. At Yoshino Palace, the emperor gathered them all and made them swear to the *kami* that they would not rebel, vowing that he himself could not live, if someone among them broke that oath. The *Nihon shoki* records that the empress also agreed to this, and the emperor surely felt relieved. A poem he wrote at this time is found in the *Man'yōshū*:

> look well at the
> goodness of good men
> and saying, it is good,
>   look well at Yoshino
> good people, look well

yoki hito no / yoshi to yoku mite / yoshi to iishi /
yoshino yoku miyo / yoki hito yoku mitsu

[MYS 1.27]

In Tenmu 10 (682), two years after the Yoshino oath,
Prince Kusakabe became crown prince. Two more years later,
Prince Ootsu, who just turned twenty-one years old, "heard
the affairs of the court for the first time," that is, he came to
actively participate in politics. For Prince Kusakabe, Prince
Ootsu's involvement was a boon, in that he had a reliable
administrative partner, but that also meant that that he could
be a strong rival. In 686, Emperor Tenmu fell ill, and two
months later, the era name was changed to "Shucho"
(literally, "red bird," both being auspicious symbols) in
prayer for his recovery. Regardless, the emperor's illness
progressed and within another month he passed away at the
age of sixty-five. Emperor Tenmu said upon his deathbed,
"Whatever the matter of this land, all should be entrusted to
the empress and the crown prince."

The Emergence of Emperor Jitō

Princess Uno Sasara (the future Emperor Jitō) had
observed the affairs of the court since Emperor Saimei's
reign. She accompanied Prince Ooama's army during the
Jinshin War. When Ooama was formally enthroned, she then

became a central figure in the court as the new empress. The *Nihon shoki* described the Empress as "composed and magnanimous." In other references, she is described as "being well-mannered and moderate, in spite of being a princess." After Uno became empress, she supported the emperor as a capable partner. When Emperor Tenmu passed away, although Prince Kusakabe was the crown prince, he did not succeed to the throne. Instead, Empress Jitō continued to administer the affairs of state. Much like her father, Emperor Tenmu, she operated under a *shōsei* system, governing political affairs without being enthroned.

The Prince Ootsu Incident

In the end, Prince Ootsu was more a rival to Crown Prince Kusakabe than an ally. Within a month of Emperor Tenmu's death, Ootsu was discovered planning a rebellion, arrested, and immediately executed. He was twenty-four years old. Compared with Kusakabe, who was a sensitive and somewhat immature nobleman, Prince Ootsu had been a sturdy, composed courtier excelling in poetry and prose and was well-respected as a frank individual. Although Prince Ootsu was her nephew, Jitō was aware that he was the only figure capable of threatening her son's position. The fact that Emperor Tenmu had taken so long to decide on Kusakabe as crown prince during his lifetime also made Jitō fear that

Prince Ootsu might be chosen as heir. The pledge of the six princes at Yoshino was likely little comfort, and so Jitō was undoubtedly the person most relieved at Prince Ootsu's death. Although Prince Ootsu had personally planned his rebellion with as many as thirty conspirators, he was still seen by many as a sympathetic figure.

Nevertheless, for Jitō, Prince Ootsu's rebellion and subsequent death marked the arrival of a new era and it is because of these troubled times that she rose to prominence. Far from being merely a question of her concerns as a mother, this was a deeply political shift in power as the throne moved from the line of her husband, Emperor Tenmu, to that of her father, Emperor Tenji. As the empress, handling this transition was a task Jitō had to oversee, and preservation of the imperial lineage was of the utmost importance.

Before Prince Ootsu's death, he and Crown Prince Kusakabe were also rivals for a woman called Ishikawa no Iratsume. Poems sent by the two princes to Iratsume survive in the *Man'yōshū*. In his poems, Prince Kusakabe openly expresses his feelings towards Iratsume [MYS 2.110], while Prince Ootsu, in his poetic exchanges with Iratsume, describes his heart humbly waiting for his loved one:

> awaiting my beloved
> in the raindrops on the
> foot-wearying mountain

Emperor Jitō   *119*

I stand being soaked in
the dripping mountain rain

ashibikino / yama no shizuku ni / imo matsu to /
ware tachi nurenu/yama no shizuku ni
[MYS 1.107]

Responding to this poem, Iratsume skillfully wrote:

as you waited for me
you must have been getting drenched —
Oh that I could be there,
in those the droplets falling
in the foot-wearying mountains

a o matsu to / kimi ga nurekun / ashibikino /
yama no shizuku ni / naramashi mono o
[MYS 1.108]

Though Ootsu and Iratsume carried out their affair in
secret, in his poem, Prince Ootsu implies he is aware that the
figure Tsumori no Muraji To'oru had revealed their tryst:

A poem written by Prince Ootsu, when the harbor
master Masuji To'oru divined that he was meeting
secretly with the young woman of Ishikawa.

when the harbor master
of the great boat
divined it, and it was
known to be true,
we two slept together

oofune no / tsumori no ura ni / noramu towa /
masashini shirite / waga futari neshi

[MYS 1.109]

This poem further suggests that Ootsu believed someone else was entangled in the affair, leading to the theory that Empress Jitō had spies keeping track of them. Prince Ootsu's writing emerged from the tension of both the empress's desire to eliminate Ootsu and Ootsu's determination to defeat his political rival, Kusakabe.

Before plotting his rebellion, Prince Ootsu secretly visited his older sister, Princess Ooku, at Ise. Having lost their mother when they were still young, they were able to trust only each other. Upon seeing her brother, who had traveled far knowing his own death might be imminent, Princess Ooku composed the following superb piece of poetry, which survives in the *Man'yōshū*:

as I see you off to Yamato,
my dear one, the night deepens

Emperor Jitō   *121*

and in the early morning dawn
I stand becoming
drenched with dew

waga seko o / yamato e yaru to / sayo fukete /
akatsuki tsuyu ni / waga tachi nureshi

[MYS 1.105]

When he faced his impending death, Prince Ootsu
composed the following *kanshi* and *waka*, which are
preserved in the *Kaifūsō* and *Man'yōshū*:

though we two were to go
together, how hard to travel
the autumn hills of Akiyama -
how are you faring, dear one,
crossing the autumn mountains all alone?

futari yukedo / yuki sugi gataki / akiyama o /
ikani ka / kimi ga hitori / koyuran

[MYS 1.106]

there are myriad wild ducks
calling on Iware pond;
is it only today
that I might see them

before vanishing in the clouds?

momotsutau / iware no ike ni / naku kamo o /
kyō nomi mite ya / kumo kakurinan

[MYS 3.416]

Princess Ooku, who hurried to the capital from Ise following her brother's death, wrote the following *waka*, lamenting his loss:

craving the sight,
my dear one, of you
who are no more,
for what reason have I come?
only to tire out my horse...

mimaku hori / waga suru kimi mo / aranaku ni /
nani shika kikemu / uma tsukaruru ni

[MYS 2.164]

This is one of four *waka* she wrote. Prince Ootsu's name has been passed down in history as a tragic figure of the ancient state.

The Enthronement of Emperor Jitō

The temporary mortuary where Emperor Tenmu's body was enshrined was kept for more than two years after his death in 686. During that time, all of the court officials who had been close associates of the emperor and even provincial administrators came to give their condolences, remembering Tenmu and praising his virtue while also pledging their loyalty to the new emperor. Thus, in Jitō 2 (688), the burial services ended as the emperor's body was interred in the imperial tumulus Asuka hinokuma oouchi. The purpose of conducting such extended funeral rites was to draw attention to the new reign. On the first day of the first month in the following year, Empress Jitō had a New Year's ceremony at the Imperial Council Hall for the first time in two years. Though she was not yet officially enthroned, it was a grand ceremony that she conducted as if she were already emperor, in the style of the previous *shōsei* system.

The court assumed that Crown Prince Kusakabe would officially ascend to the throne. However, in the fourth month of 689, Kusakabe passed away suddenly. He was twenty-eight years old. His consort was Princess Ahe (the later Emperor Genmei), daughter of Emperor Tenji, and together they had a seven-year old son, Prince Karu. The death of Prince Kusakabe was a shock to Empress Jitō even greater than Emperor Tenmu's death. Despite her scrupulous efforts to ensure that her own son would become emperor and her bloodline would protect the imperial throne, all her efforts came to naught. It was customary that if a crown prince had not been chosen at the time of an emperor's death that the empress should be selected. Thus, Empress Jitō, who had already been ruling behind the scenes, was enthroned as Emperor Takamagahara hiro no hime no sumera mikoto, the new Emperor Jitō.

Emperor Jitō had observed court politics with her own eyes since she was a young girl under the reign of her father, Emperor Tenji, and after she was married, with her husband Prince Ooama. As the empress, she always accompanied Emperor Tenmu, and after his death, she was directly involved in political matters. There was nothing to stand in the way of her administering affairs of state. She was surrounded with capable staff and there were no powerful figures challenging her, allowing her reign to proceed smoothly.

In 689, a year before her enthronement, the Asuka Kiyomihara Codes were completed and promulgated. Although the content of these ordinances does not survive, they became the foundation for the later Taihō Codes. They consisted largely of regulations related to central administration, taxation, and provincial administration. The *Nihon shoki* states that "the Eight Ministries, Hundred Offices, and all others moved [to the capital,]" demonstrating the increasingly centralized organization of government offices. Prince Takechi was appointed as First Minister of the Great Council of State, the top position, and Tajihino shima no mahito was made Minister of the Right. The role of First Minister was second only to that of crown prince, and when there was no crown prince, First Ministers undertook those duties. With the death of Crown Prince Kusakabe, the Emperor Jitō lost her closest ally, and her grandson, Prince Karu, was the most appropriate choice for successor. Prince Karu, however, was too young to fulfill the role, and it seemed most reasonable that Prince Takechi, who had performed meritoriously during the Jinshin War, should succeed her. The emperor, however, was still uneasy. If something happened to her, the imperial throne, which she had worked so hard to keep within her own family lineage, might go to another. Even so, her reign continued without incident.

As for the tax system reforms, in 690, taxation by household was replaced with the taxation of individuals under a renewed census process known as *kōin nenjaku*.[45] The military system was also reformed, requiring one conscript per household, and administrative divisions such as province (*kuni*), district/county (*gun*), and village (*ri*) were established. Local chieftains known as *kuni no miyatsuko* who had

---

[45] The term *kōin nenjaku* 庚寅年籍 refers to *kōin*, the sexagenary zodiac year for 690, and *nenjaku*, referring to the annual register.

previously managed local areas were soon joined or replaced by *kokushi*, provincial governors dispatched by the central government. With this, a state wielding centralized power with the emperor at its center was well underway.

As the administration system was more or less completed, a new capital was needed as a base of operations. A flat area of land known as Yamato *sanzan*, literally "the three mountains of Yamato," encompassed by Mt. Kagu, Mt. Unebi, and Mt. Miminashi, was chosen as a proposed site for the capital, and Prince Takechi went to survey it. The emperor also went to view the site herself in the twelfth month of that year. With an enormous amount of resources, both financial as well as human, the new palace was completed, and the emperor transferred her residence there in the twelfth month of Jitō 8 (694). Known as the Fujiwara Palace, this location remained the capital until it was relocated to Heijō. The *Man'yōshū* includes two *waka* describing the construction of the Fujiwara Palace.[46]

Along with the palace, the aforementioned construction of Yakushiji Temple was another large-scale project that took place in this time period. Emperor Tenmu had originally proposed the construction of Yakushiji Temple with the

---

[46] One of them was said to have been composed by a corvee (unpaid) laborer involved in the palace's construction (MYS 1.50), while another other was entitled "Poem of the Fujiwara Palace Well" (MYS 1.52, 1.53, Author unknown).

express purpose of praying for Empress Jitō's recovery from an illness.[47] However, it remained unfinished. Although the details are unclear, *Nihon shoki* records that the eye-opening ceremony for the Yakushi Buddha[48] enshrined in the temple was performed in 697. The temple in its entirety was not completed until Monmu 2 (698).

Articles on Emperor Jitō in the *Nihon shoki* do not suggest any particular disturbances during her reign. Starting at the new year, there are a number of articles on various official and ceremonial occasions, such as conferment of ranks and merits, appointments to offices, exemptions from taxation, special rations, pardons, and banquets.[49] Regulations were placed on the dress of court officials, and diplomatic exchanges, too, were closely regulated, with those who arrived in Japan from Shiragi and Kudara (Koma had been destroyed in 660) being assigned to various provinces and treated in the same manner as Japanese officials. Specialists in music, writing, medicine, and ritual magic were also treated

---

[47] The Yakushi Buddha, or Medicine Buddha, is a deity that was often prayed to in order to cure illness.

[48] The eye-opening ceremony is so-named because a priest was called upon to paint in the pupils of the great Buddha statue, thus symbolically bringing it to life.

[49] One interesting case of special ration distribution was one in which twenty bundles of rice plants were given to people over eighty years old living in the Kinai region, and twenty bundles of rice plants were also granted to 5,300 other elderly people.

with respect, all of which demonstrated the great lengths to which the emperor went to advance the domestic culture. Compared to previous reigns, life was uneventful. In such a peaceful era, the only conspicuous events were Emperor Jito's frequent visits to Yoshino.

Jitō's Visits to Yoshino

The first reference to an emperor's visit to the Yoshino villa is found in the Emperor Ōjin (r. 270-310) section of the *Nihon shoki*. During the reign of Emperor Saimei, it is said that "the Yoshino villa was built," though this may have been a new construction. The Yoshino referred to in these descriptions is not the so-called "Mt. Yoshino with cherry blossoms," an epithet often seen in classical poetry, but is thought to be the area around Miyataki, modern day Yoshino in Nara prefecture. References found in the *Nihon shoki* alone record Emperor Jitō visiting Yoshino thirty-one times in eleven years, including during her period of *shōsei* rule. She once visited there even as retired emperor after abdicating the throne. Including the two occasions when she visited with Emperor Monmu (r. 697-707) on his trips, Jitō traveled to Yoshino three times after her retirement. These were too many visits to be simply for recuperation; it seems more likely that she had obligations there or a particular place or thing to which she was attracted. Although the *Nihon shoki* simply records the dates on which the emperor came and went from Yoshino, according to those articles, the Emperor Jitō's visits can be summarized as follows:

Emperor Jitō first began to visit Yoshino in the first month of the Jito 3 (689) and she visited Yoshino twice in that year. In three separate years, 690 (the year of her enthronement), 693, and 695, she traveled to Yoshino as many as five times. The year she abdicated the throne (697) she visited once. During many other years, she went to Yoshino three or four times, which was quite frequent. Jitō traveled to Yoshino most often in the fourth month, and in all those visits, only once in the ninth month. Otherwise, her travel times varied. Her longest stay was for nineteen days, and most visits lasted between seven to eleven days, with very few being as short as two or three. It appears that there was no particular pattern to the times at which she departed for Yoshino or returned. Some theorize that Jitō had a particular fondness for Yoshino because it was the place where her husband, worried about his successor, gathered the princes and conducted the Yoshino Oath, the place where he cloistered himself after taking the tonsure, and the place from which he raised his army for the Jinshin War. However, there may be other reasons why this female emperor traveled to Yoshino so frequently, including religious reasons. One theory is that her visits might have been related to the Wind Festival of Tatsuta Shrine or the Daikijin Festival of Hirose

Shrine, both of which were started during her reign. In fact, the emperor sent messengers to those festivals while she was in the mountains of Yoshino. These two shrines were located in the western part of present-day Nara prefecture, directly to the northwest of Yoshino.

Since many of the records only record Jitō's date of departure, nothing definitive can be said as to whether or not there was a special meaning to her frequent visits to Yoshino in the fourth month and at the beginning of months. Since the *Nihon shoki* does not record how she spent her days in Yoshino, it is unknown whether she was there simply for rest or for a more specific purpose.[50] Whatever the reasons, her extended time away from the capital, which was somewhat unusual, suggests that Yoshino was a place with special meaning to Emperor Jitō.

A large number of people typically accompanied the emperor during her travels, and among them was the famed poet Kakinomoto no Hitomaro. Although little is known of his background, a large number of his celebrated poems recorded in the *Man'yōshu* have assured his legacy as one of the great poets of his time. A poet of the court, he wrote *waka*

---

[50] Torquil Duthie suggests that Yoshino had a special association with Emperor Tenmu's divine authority vis-à-vis the worship of the sun goddess at Ise. Thus, for Jitō, frequent visits to Yoshino may have been a legitimizing act that emphasized historical continuity in the imperial line. Duthie, 273.

Emperor Jitō   *131*

dedicated to Princess Kusakabe and Prince Takechi as well as many other princes and princesses. The following poem was dedicated to Emperor Jitō on the occasion of one of her visits to Yoshino:

> A poem written by Lord Kakinomoto no Hitomaro when he had the good fortune to be at the palace in Yoshino

> Our great Sovereign
> rules in peace
> all the lands under heaven
> although there are many,
> among all the clear pools
> of the mountain streams,
> it is Yoshino which
> draws her heart,
> the clear plains of Akitsu
> where the cherry blossoms fall
> and since she built
> the sturdy pillars of her palace here,
> the men of the great palace
> align their boats
> to cross the morning river
> race their boats
> to cross the evening river

her palace is eternal as the river
lofty as the mountains
however often she sees them
she never tires
of the rushing water of the waterfall
beside the palace

I never weary of beholding
the water moss of
    Yoshino river
which grows unceasing —
    I will return to gaze again

yasumishishi / wago ookimi no / kikoshimesu /
    ame no shita ni / kuni wa shimo /
sawani aredomo / yama kawa no / kiyoki kawachi to /
    mikokoro o /
yoshino no kuni no / hana chirau/akitsu no nobe ni /
    miyahashira / futoshiki maseba / momoshikino /
oomiyabito wa / fune namete / asa kawa watari / fune kisoi /
yūkawa wataru / kono kawa no / tayuru koto naku /
    kono yama no /
iya taka shirazu / mizu tagitsu / taki no miyako wa /
    miredo akanu kamo

miredo akanu / yoshino no kawa no / tokoname no /

Emperor Jitō   *133*

tayuru koto naku / mata kaeri min

[MYS 1.36-37]

The envoy poem following the main verses praises the beauty of the Yoshino villa.

The *Man'yōshū* also contains *waka* composed by Emperor Jitō herself. One of them is well-known as one of the hundred poems collected in the *Hyakunin isshu*. The *Man'yōshū* also contains *chōka* and two *waka* she composed at the time of Emperor Tenmu's death. One of the *waka* is as follows:

> the blue clouds
> in the clouds trailing down
> from the northern hills
> leave behind the stars,
> leave behind the moon

kitayama ni / tanabiku kumo no / seiun no /
hoshi sakari yuki / tsuki o sakarite

[MYS 2.161]

This poem is a cathartic one, describing Tenmu's spirit growing distant from the empress and his children left behind as it becomes a cloud trailing in the sky. Due to the strictness of poetic conventions, it was rare in this period for *waka* other

134

than seasonal poems about Tanabata[51] to contain imagery about the stars. This may suggest that imported Chinese cosmological practices had begun to gain wider acceptance in Japan. The following poem, which is written in a somewhat playful fashion, is also thought to have been written by Jitō, demonstrating her intelligence and quick wit.

> Although I said stop!
> and just did not listen
> to old Shii's insistent talk,
> now I find myself
> yearning for it

> ina to iedo / shiuru shii noga shiigatari /
> konogoro kikazu te / ware koini keri

[MYS 3.236]

In eighth month of Jitō 11 (697), Emperor Jitō abdicated the throne to her fifteen-year-old grandson, Prince Karu (Emperor Monmu), and administered affairs of state with him

---

[51] Tanabata, or the Star Festival, is a celebration that typically takes place on the seventh day of the seventh month and marks the meeting of the stars Vega and Altair, known in Japanese folklore as the deities Orihime (the Weaver) and Hikoboshi (the Oxherder), who meet on a bridge of magpies (the Milky Way).

as the new emperor. She also enthusiastically worked to complete the Taihō *ritsuryō* codes, which were issued to all the provinces on the fourteenth day of the tenth month. The completion of these administrative codes tentatively brought an end to her involvement in affairs of state, so Retired Emperor Jitō then went to inspect the province of Mikawa, which she had long wanted to visit. She returned to the palace in the eleventh month, after having visited the provinces of Owari, Mino, Ise, and Iga. During her time as emperor, when the Fujiwara Palace was being built, Jitō had traveled to Ise during harvest season, despite objections from the court. Both instances illustrate Emperor Jitō's assertive character. However, she was quite old by the time of that distant journey, and in the twelfth month of that year, she fell ill. In spite of amnesty grants for the sake of prayers for her recovery, hundreds of people becoming priests, and recitations of the Golden Light Sutra (*konkōmyō-kyō*) in the four provinces around the capital, her tumultuous life ended on the twenty-second day of the twelfth month in Taihō 2 (702). Jitō was fifty-eight years old. Her last request was that people of the court should continue their work in regular clothes as usual, and that her funeral should be plain and simple. According to the *Shoku Nihongi*, the temporary mortuary where her body was enshrined remained for a year, and her body was cremated in Asuka no Oka on the seventeenth day of the twelfth month of Taiho 3. It was the first time in history that an emperor was cremated, and her ashes were buried together with Emperor Tenmu in the Hinokuma Oouchi tumulus. Jitō's reign as retired emperor had lasted for just over four years.

Column 3

The Inner Palace system was arranged according to status

The Inner Palace (*kōkyū*) refers to those women of the imperial court who are not involved with shrine rituals, such as the priestess of the Ise Shrine. The official wife of the emperor was the empress, and there were three other titles for consorts; *hi*, *bunin*, and *hin*, each of which showed the social status of the woman's family. The number of the women for each title was also fixed. There were typically two *hi*, who were from the imperial family, three *bunin/fujin*, who were above the third rank, and four *hin*, who were daughters of families above the fifth rank. Other women were simply referred to as palace staff. In the early years of the Heian period, the titles changed, and *chūgū*, *nyōgo*, *kōi*, and *miyasudokoro* came to refer to the emperor's consorts.

Emperor Genmei
(r. 707-715)

Translated by Hiroko Manabe

A reserved female emperor who
cared deeply for her people.

The Enthronement of Emperor Genmei

Emperor Genmei was the fifth female emperor. The Nara period (710-794) began with her reign. Genmei was Emperor Tenji's fourth daughter, Princess Ahe. Her mother was Mei no Iratsume, daughter of Soga Yamada Ishikawa no maro, and so she was Emperor Jitō's half-sister. Princess Ahe was married to Prince Kusakabe, the son of Emperor Tenmu and Jitō, and with Kusakabe she had a son, Prince Karu. As stated in the previous chapter, Prince Kusakabe, as the crown prince, was expected to inherit the throne. But with his sudden death, Emperor Tenmu's empress was enthroned and became Emperor Jitō. She took part in state affairs until her grandson and Genmei's son, Prince Karu, came of age. When he turned fifteen years old, she stepped down and Prince Karu ascended to the throne to become Emperor

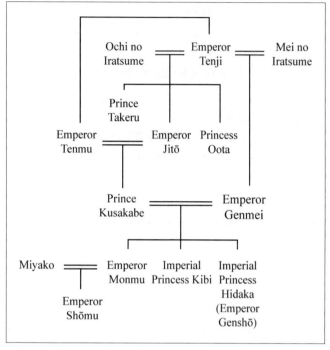

Lineage of Emperor Genmei

Monmu. Like his father, the late Prince Kusakabe, the new emperor was a delicate young man and a modest leader. He died at the age of twenty-four, having reigned for only ten years. Monmu had a son, Prince Obito (701-756), with Miyako, the daughter of Fujiwara no Fuhito, but Obito was seven years old when Monmu died. The emperor also had two sisters, the Princesses Hidaka and Kibi, but no brothers. His grandfather, Emperor Tenmu, had many sons, some of whom

Emperor Genmei

still enjoyed good health, and may have had an eye on the throne. Monmu, in order to preserve his own lineage, had no other choice than to enthrone his mother, Princess Ahe, so as his own health deteriorated, he asked her to ascend to the throne. This is how Ahe became Emperor Genmei. Her reign was a way to buy time, protecting the throne until the young prince came of age. Emperor Saimei ascended to the throne for her son, Emperor Tenji in a similar manner. Both Emperors Saimei and Genmei were thus meant to rule as intermediaries.

Many texts considered foundational works of Japanese history were created during this time period. The historical text *Nihon shoki* details the period from Japan's mythological "Age of the Gods" to Emperor Jitō's era, and was the first historical chronicle to be compiled by imperial command. Prince Toneri, Emperor Tenmu's son, spearheaded its compilation and it was completed in Yōrō 4 (720). The next major chronicle, *Shoku Nihongi*, was published in forty volumes, covering the niney-five years from the beginning of Emperor Monmu's reign, Monmu 1 (697), to Emperor Kanmu's reign, Enryaku 10 (791). The *Shoku Nihongi* therefore covered the entirety of the Nara period. After many setbacks and complications, the history was completed in Enryaku 16 (797). Following the completion of the *Shoku Nihongi*, four more histories were created in succession: *Nihon kōki, Shoku Nihon kōki, Nihon Montoku Tennō jitsuroku,*

140

and *Nihon sandai jitsuroku.* These six compilations are collectively called *Rikkokushi* (The Six National Histories). They are the only historical collections in Japan produced by imperial command, and no further national history books of this kind have been produced by imperial order since.

The Era of Emperor Monmu

There were no noteworthy crises during the ten years of Emperor Monmu's reign. The emperor was known to be a mild-mannered man who never lost his temper. He enjoyed studying the teachings of Confucius and history texts. He was also described as a talented archer. The most important event of this period was the promulgation of the Taihō Code. The courtier Fujiwara no Fuhito expanded upon and consolidated the Asuka Kiyomihara Code that had been established in Emperor Tenmu's reign, creating what became known as the Taihō Code. Around the same time, the imperial court received an offering of gold from Tsushima, and so, in commemoration of the proclamation of the new laws and the gift, the era name was changed to "Taihō." It is likely that the retired Emperor Jitō actively supported the young Emperor Monmu throughout the period of the Taihō Code's establishment.

In the first month of Taihō 1 (701), prior to the issuance of the new statutes, it was decided, after a lapse of thirty-one years, to resume sending delegates to the T'ang Dynasty. Awata no Mahito was appointed as an envoy plenipotentiary (*shissetsushi*), and was given a special sword from the emperor to carry with him on the mission, during which he was invested with full diplomatic representation of the court. Though he held no rank, the poet Yamanoue no Okura was also selected as an official member of the envoy mission. Their trip to China was postponed for a year due to typhoons, but they left in the following year and came back two years later in Keiun 1 (704). While in China, Okura wrote the following poem:

> okay, let's go, fellows!
> let's hurry up off to Yamato —
> the pine beach in Mitsu
> at Ootomo must be pining
> waiting for us!

iza kodomo / hayaku yamato e / ootomo no /
mitsu no Hamamatsu / machi koinu ran

[MYS 1.63]

The *Shoku Nihongi,* being an imperial history, is primarily comprised of official accounts and rarely contains any episodic stories. One account that stands out, however, is that of the well-known priest, Dōshō, who founded the Hossō

Sect during the Asuka period. When Dōshō traveled to the continent, he studied Buddhism under the Sanzō priest Genjō,[52] who told Dōshō about his travels to western China. He advised Dōshō to study Zen when he returned to Japan. Before his death, Dōshō's last wish was to be cremated; he was purportedly the first person in Japan to have ever been cremated. Emperor Jitō, too, was later cremated according to her final wishes. Another interesting episode among the more formal accounts concerns En no Gyōja (also known as En no Ozunu). According to the records, he pursued ascetic practices in the mountains of Yoshino and Oomine, eventually mastering mystical powers. He established *shugendō* and propagated its practice among the people.[53] He was later sent into exile in Izu for abducting people.

The Era of Emperor Genmei

In Keiun 3 (706). 11, Emperor Monmu fell ill. He attempted to pass the throne to his mother, the Empress Dowager, but she refused. Emperor Monmu died in the sixth

---

[52] *Sanzō* 三蔵 is the designation given to priests who have mastered 1) Buddhist scriptures, 2) Buddhist laws and 3) discourses on the first two.

[53] *Shugendō* 修験道 is a syncretic, ascetic practice originating in Japanese folk customs relating to worship of the natural world.

month of the following year. Prince Obito was only seven years old at the time, and there was no one else eligible who could maintain the imperial line except for Emperor Monmu's mother. Thus, the forty-third emperor, Yamato Neko Amatsu Mishiro Toyokuni Narihime, also known as Emperor Genmei, was enthroned.

On Keiun 4 (707).6.24, the new Emperor Genmei arrived in the east wing of the palace and conveyed Monmu's last wishes that she should accede to the throne to the court officials. The coronation was held in the fall, on Keiun 4.7. 17, in the Imperial Council Hall. In her inaugural proclamation, she stressed the importance of the continuity of the imperial line, and, in the beginning of her speech, referred back to Emperor Tenji, who once stated that the imperial line was "as old as heaven and earth, as long as time immemorial, a principle that must not be altered." In accordance with that very law, Emperor Jitō had previously assumed the throne and in time relinquished it to Crown Prince Karu, the Emperor Monmu, when he came of age. Genmei stated that she now ascended the throne in keeping with that immutable, enduring law.

According to historians, Emperor Tenji may have eliminated a provision in the Ōmi Code dictating that in order to become emperor, one's mother must be of imperial blood and determined that the candidate instead must be a legitimate child; it is likely that this was done so his favorite son, Prince

144

Ootomo, could succeed to the throne. Emperor Genmei, who awaited Prince Obito's maturity and acted as guardian of the imperial succession, referred to that precedent set by Emperor Jitō. In other words, Emperor Genmei would serve as an intermediary.

However, one notable aspect of her reign was that, in contrast to her predecessors, Emperor Genmei issued a large number of imperial decrees. Seldom recorded in the *Nihon shoki,* they appear in great numbers in the *Shoku Nihongi.* Though this may be because of the intentions of its editors, during the eight years of Emperor Genmei's reign, a considerable number of imperial decrees were recorded. Though most were about mundane matters such as the conferring of posthumous honors, rewards, amnesty and prohibitions, some were not so conventional. The decree proclaimed in Wadō 1 (708). 8, for example, mandated detailed clothing regulations, such as the size of sleeve cuffs and the width of neckbands. However, the most significant proclamations of this era were the announcement of *Wadōkaichin* currency and the transfer of the capital to Heijō.

Wadōkaichin

On Keiun 5 (708). 1. 11, a year after her coronation, copper was presented to the court from the Chichibu district of Musashi province. Emperor Genmei promptly issued an

Emperor Genmei   *145*

imperial edict roughly as follows:

> From the time of the descent of the Sun Goddess'
> grandson from Takamagahara until now, all the
> succeeding emperors, as descendants of the Sun
> Goddess, have reigned over this land and loved the
> people. As I myself took the throne, I paid reverence
> to the heaven and the earth. Recently, it was reported
> that copper was found in the eastern province of
> Musashi, and it was offered in tribute to the court. I
> believe this to be a blessing sent by the *kami* of the
> heavens and *kami* of the earth who were pleased with
> the emperors' reigns. To commemorate this god-sent
> treasure, I declare that the era name be changed to
> Wadō.[54] This year, the fifth year of Keiun, will
> become the first year of Wadō.

In other words, the discovery of copper was a particularly
auspicious event. Not only was the era name changed, but
conferment of rank, reward giving, exemptions from taxation,
and amnesties were carried out in honor of this occasion.

For the administration, this tribute of copper was much

---

[54] The characters for *Wadō* 和銅 are 和, referring to peace,
harmony, or Yamato (大和), and 銅, meaning copper.

more than a formal gift from a subject. Wasting no time, in the second month, they appointed the first official, *Saijusenshi* (literally "Chief of Coin Casting"), who would administer the minting of coins. On the twenty-sixth day of the seventh month, the first copper coins were minted in Ōmi province. These coins were called *Wadōkaichin*. Some of them have been excavated and preserved. They each are 2.4 cm in diameter and weigh about 3.75 grams. There is a square hole in the center around which four characters, wa (和), *dō* (同), *kai* (開) and *chin* (珎) are engraved. This currency came into use in the eighth month. Prior to these copper coins, silver coins had also been produced, but were discontinued in the following year.

With this, the economy began to shift from a goods-based system to a monetary system. However, this system was not without challenges: as early as the first month of the following year, Wadō 2, another imperial proclamation was issued regarding counterfeiting. People were beginning to cast their own copper coins in secret and enter them into circulation, and so the emperor stated that those who forged coins and used them would be punished. In Wadō 3, Dazaifu and Harima province presented copper coins to the court.

In the fifth month of Wadō 4 (711), the administration fixed the price of unhulled rice to encourage the exchanging goods for currency. Additionally, in the tenth month, salary regulations were created stating that government employees be paid partially in coin currency. This perplexed some employees, who had never seen coins before. Another subsequent provision was the *Chikusen joi ryō,* or "Law for Conferment of Ranks according to the Amount of Money Amassed," which stated that those who saved the coins would be promoted to higher ranks in proportion to the amount they saved. This provision also included penal regulations against the production of counterfeit money. At the end of Wadō 5, they could now pay their taxes with coins instead of the traditional way of paying with local products (*chō*) or with labor (*yō*). It was reported that the eight provinces surrounding the Kinai could take as long as ten years to pay their taxes, and other local provinces may have taken much longer. Nevertheless, *Wadōkaichin* began to gradually circulate, and it was used until *Mannen tsūhō* coins replaced it in Tenpyō hōji 4 (760).

The Heijō Capital

It was common practice to relocate the capital when a new emperor was enthroned. However, from the beginning of his reign, Emperor Monmu administered affairs of state from the Fujiwara Palace, as his grandmother, Emperor Jitō, had done. In Keiun 4 (707).2 Emperor Monmu issued an imperial decree that the capital should be moved, and had the princes

148

and officials above fifth rank deliberate on the matter. He died before they could come to a conclusion, and the issue of moving the capital was abandoned.

In Wadō 1 (708), Emperor Genmei issued a decree concerning the transfer of the capital. The content was as follows:

> The idea that "the people who build a palace endure hardships while the people who reside there live in comfort" has weighed on my mind, so I was reluctant to move the capital in haste. Those around me have reminded me that from ancient times, the emperor's rule was established by deciding where to place the capital through examining the sun and the stars to determine the foundations for the imperial palace, divining their circumstances, and using geomancy. They tell me that by undertaking those procedures, the emperor can secure the land and continue the imperial line forever. I cannot ignore their concerns, and find their sentiments compelling. The capital is indeed the center of all government offices and a place where people come together from far and wide. It is not my personal domain. Therefore, I must transfer the capital if I find somewhere more suitable than Fujiwara for its functions. It is written that the kings of the Yin Dynasty transferred the capital five times and

consequently reconstructed the country. During the Zhou Dynasty, the kings relocated the capital three times, which brought about peace. Given these precedents, I am gratified, and I believe I shall move our capital.

Then, she continued to explain why the Heijō site was an appropriate location:

Heijō is perfectly situated *(shikin zu ni kanau)*. Three mountains, Mt. Kagu, Mt. Miminashi and Mt. Unebi, protect the southern region. Its geomantic positioning is ideal. We must set up our capital in Heijō.

She added this thoughtful consideration:

As for the building materials, itemize them and report to the throne. Build the roads and bridges in the fall after the harvest season. Make it so the people can enjoy coming there. Lay the plans wisely so as not to have troubles later.

The words s*hikin zu ni kanau* are often used in relation to archaeological excavation in Asuka and its vicinity. *Shikin* refers to the Chinese principles of cosmic dual forces, which

150

include the four celestial creatures: blue dragon, white tiger, red bird and black tortoise entwined with a snake, which are auspiciously associated with the east, west, south and north, respectively. *Zu* refers to the the topography and *ni kanau* means to be suitable to. In Heijō, there was a river in the east, a road in the west, a pond in the south and a mountain in the north. This is considered a very favorable topography according to divinatory practices, giving the location an ideal configuration.

The establishment of new capitals was highly influenced by the T'ang Dynasty, and the new capital was constructed emulating the model of Chang'an, the T'ang capital. The imperial palace was built in the center of a rectangular site, which ran about 4.3 km from east to west and 4.8 km from north to south. It was enclosed by roofed mud-walls (*rajō*), and had twelve gates. Within the walls, a main road known as *Suzaku-ōji* (literally, "The Great Avenue of the Red Bird") ran from north to south dividing the city into two sections: Sakyō (the left capital) and Ukyō (the right capital). Each section had streets running from east to west and from north to south. Government offices were placed at the corners of the streets. Outside the palace walls there were lots, called *bō*, for temples and aristocrats' residences. The site of Heijō Palace was slightly southeast of what is now the city of Nara.

The Heijō capital was called Nara no miyako. The name

itself can be inscribed in various ways with Chinese characters. In the *Man'yōshū*, Nara is written in five ways: 奈羅, 那羅, 乃楽, 諾楽, and 寧楽. There are many theories as to the origin of the name. One suggests that the name was derived from the *nara* tree which grew abundantly in the area, while another points to how soldiers about to engage their enemies stamped the earth with their feet (*fumi nara shita*). Heijō occupied primarily flat country with the gently sloping Mt. Nara in the north. The south was wide open with a view of the faraway Asuka region.

On the fourteenth day of the ninth month, Emperor Genmei journeyed to Sugawara (a section of what is now Nara), and on the twentieth day, she visited Heijō to inspect the site of the new capital. Continuing her trip, she stayed at imperial villas in Okada and Kasuga in Yamashiro province before returning to the Fujiwara capital on the twenty-eighth. The trip took two weeks. Satisfied with her preliminary inspection, on the thirtieth, Genmei appointed Abe no Sukunamaro and Tajihi no Mahito Ikemori to be the administrators of the Heijō capital's construction and selected other personnel as well. On the second day of the tenth month, the emperor made an offering of cloth (*heihaku*) to Ise Shrine and reported the construction plans of Heijō Palace to the enshrined deity. Thus, all was in order for the establishment of the new capital, and a ceremony to purify the site was held on the fifth day of the twelfth month.

152

In Wadō 2 (709). 8, Emperor Genmei once again inspected the construction site. She returned to the Fujiwara capital on the fifth day of the ninth month, but prior to this she showed her appreciation for the people who had toiled in the construction by conferring court ranks, presenting imperial gifts, and exempting them from taxes. She also showed her sympathetic consideration to the public. On the eleventh day of the tenth month, she ordered the chief of the construction that, in event of an old tomb being unearthed, the workers should bury it as before, consecrate it with rice wine, and appease the spirit of the deceased enshrined there. Genmei then issued a decree stating:

> The relocation of the capital is causing much distress to the people, whose lives have been uprooted. I do not want them to suffer further, so they will be exempted from paying their taxes this year.

These episodes reveal the emperor's concern over how transferring the capital could place heavy burdens on ordinary people. She visited Heijō again in the twelfth month.

The following year, in Wadō 3 (710), construction was finished and the capital was moved to Heijō.[55] The Minister of

---

[55] The year 2010 was the 1,300th anniversary of the Heijō capital.

Emperor Genmei   *153*

the Left, Isonokami no Ason Maro, remained at Fujiwara
Palace to take charge there. In *Man'yōshū* we find the poem
Emperor Genmei composed at the time:

> if I take my leave
> from the village of Asuka
> of the soaring birds,
> am I never more to see
> the place where you remain?

tobu tori no / asuka no sato o / okite inaba /
kimi ga atari wa / miezu kamo aran

[MYS 1.78]

The introduction to the poem tells when and where it was
created: "On a spring day in the second month of Wadō 3, on
her way to Nara from Fujiwara, Emperor Genmei stopped the
palanquin at Nagaya no hara, looked back toward the old
capital, and wrote this poem." It is full of sentiment for her
old palace. With this, the Nara Period, praised as "glorious
like a full blossom,"[56] began. It lasted for seven generations,
from Wadō 3 (710) through Enryaku 3 (784). Emperor

---

[56] This phrase was taken from the famous *waka* by Ono no Oyu
(MYS 3.328).

Genmei was at the forefront, guiding the grand enterprise that was the Heijō capital and its era. The *Shoku Nihongi* includes a number of detailed accounts related to the after-effects of the capital's establishment. It was reported that many laborers from various provinces fled from the construction site due to overwork and that guard houses were ordered to be built to protect the armories, as the walls of the new capital were not yet finished. Also noted was Genmei's decree commanding provincial administrators to supply laborers returning home with sufficient provisions for the journey, and that if some of them should perish from starvation, to carefully report those deaths to their home provinces for census purposes.

There is no question that the most important event of Emperor Genmei's reign was the transfer of the capital to Heijō. Although it is not recorded in the *Shoku Nihongi* (which was completed in 797), the compilation of the iconic *Kojiki*, the oldest extant record of Japanese history, was completed in Wadō 5 (712). Histories of this period record in detail a variety of generous imperial decrees, such as tax exemptions, conferment of court rank, stipend increases, exemption from labor services, measures for the old and the poor, special ration allotments, amnesties, charity, but also a great deal of punitive provisions. It is difficult to determine how these edicts reflect Genmei's personal initiatives and how many were simply routine matters of state.

Emperor Genmei   *155*

After the relocation, Emperor Genmei often vacationed at the imperial villa in Mikanohara rather than Yoshino, which Emperor Jitō had frequented. Mikanohara was in Yamashiro province (what is now Kamochō, Sōraku district, Kyoto) and in the time of Emperor Shōmu, it became the Kuni capital. It was surely one of her only times to rest away from the hectic affairs of state. Just after Genmei took the throne in Wadō 1, she wrote the following poem, which was recorded in *Man'yōshū*:

> the wrist guards
> of the steadfast soldiers thrum;
> the warrior lords
> must all be standing
> by their upright shields

masurao no / tomo no oto sunari / mononou no /
oomaetsu kimi tate tatsu rashimo

[MYS 1.76]

This poem may suggest that she, as emperor, felt uneasy as she heard the movement of soldiers for the first time. Her elder sister, Princess Minabe, responded to this apprehension:

> O my great lord,
> fear not!

the gods of our land
will continue to bless us
and we will never disappear

waga ookii / mono na omooshi / sumekami no /
tsugite tamaeru / ware nakenaku ni

[MYS 1.77]

She encouraged her sister with heartfelt sympathy. From that day, Emperor Genmei felt the full weight of her position. But the occasion drew nearer when that burden would ease.

On Wadō 7 (714). 6. 25, Prince Obito turned fourteen years old and his coming of age ceremony was held. On New Year's Day the following year, Reiki 1, he made his entrance at the New Year's celebration in full court dress. At that moment, auspicious clouds formed in the sky and Emperor Genmei immediately issued a declaration that court ranks and amnesties should be conferred.

Transference of the Throne from Mother to Daughter

On the second day of the ninth month, Emperor Genmei suddenly vacated the throne to allow Princess Hidaka to ascend. Genmei released the following statement:

I, as the emperor, have ruled over the country and cared for the people by the grace of Heaven. The country is governed well and peacefully, thanks to the virtue inherited generation after generation from my ancestors. I have set my heart on the reverence of the heavens and my ancestors day and night without fail. I have worried and pored over the affairs of state for nine years. Now, my youth has gradually faded, and as I age, I grow weary of politics. I would like to live a peaceful and quiet life, as free as the clouds and the wind. I will forsake all worldly connections, as if taking off my shoes. I desire to cede the Sacred Treasures, the symbols of the Imperial House, to the Crown Prince, but he is still too young to leave the palace. However, the affairs of state cannot be neglected for even a day. Princess Hidaka has possessed intelligence from her earliest years and is broad-minded and compassionate by nature. She is serious, young, and beautiful. She also has a good reputation among the people. They will certainly admire her.

With this, her daughter became Emperor Genshō, and Genmei became the retired emperor. Histories from Genshō's time do not give many accounts of what became of Genmei after she relinquished the throne. However, when she became ill in Yōrō 5 (721), Emperor Genshō issued an imperial decree on the sixth day of the fifth month, declaring her wish to devote herself to Buddhism and to pray for her sick mother. This declaration inspired many of her subordinates and ordinary people to also become devoted Buddhists. The Retired Emperor Genmei's condition worsened, however, and on the thirteenth day of the tenth month, Genmei summoned the Minister of the Right, Prince Nagaya, and Imperial Advisor, Fujiwara no Fusasaki, and delivered her dying wish:

> All living things must die. When I am deceased, do not have a pompous funeral for me that will disrupt the lives of the people, with all the officials dressed gaudily. When I die, build a furnace at the summit of Mt. Nara in the north of Mt. Saho in the Soegami district of Yamato province and cremate me. Bury my ashes there. My posthumous title shall be simply "Emperor Who Governed the Court in This Place." On the day of the funeral, the emperor should attend to state affairs as usual, as should the imperial family members and government officials. Do not let them escort the coffin: have the police and guards take strict precautions and be ready for any accident or emergency.

Emperor Genmei   *159*

Moreover, she issued a decree the next day requesting a modest and quiet funeral service, and gave detailed instructions for it. On the twenty-fourth day of the tenth month, she summoned Fujiwara no Fusasaki again, and asked him to support Emperor Genshō and to work together for the peace and security of the country in whatever situations might arise. Emperor Genmei was an unassuming and modest emperor, who considered the people's well-being more important than anything else. On the seventh day of the twelfth month in 721, she died at the age of sixty-one in the Heijō palace. As she had requested, there was an unpretentious funeral for her. On the thirteenth day, her ashes were buried in the imperial tomb in Mt. Nara.

Column 4

Policies for the elderly in the Nara Period

The imperial edicts of Emperor Genmei, Emperor Genshō, and Emperor Kōken occasionally show consideration for the aged. For example, special rations of millet were given to the elderly residents of the capital: people over one hundred years of age were given an amount of two *koku,* those over ninety, one *koku* and five *to,* and those over eighty, one *koku.*[57] At other times, rations of *ashiginu* (silk woven with thick strands) were distributed in the same way. The total population in Japan during the Nara Period was about 6,000,000 people, while the capital had about 200,000. In Hōki 4 (773), the number of elderly in the capital who were provided special rations was recorded as two people over one hundred years old, 104 people over ninety years old, and 190 over eighty years old. In comparison, in 2005 the total population of Japan was 120,000,000, and Tokyo had about 12,000,000 people. In the whole country, there are 20,000 people over one hundred years old, about one million over ninety years old, and about 25,000,000 over sixty-five years old.[58]

---

[57] Although it is difficult to know the exact measurements that were used, one *koku* may have been about 180 liters, and one *koku* was equivalent to 10 *to.*

[58] 2015 statistics place the population of Japan at approximately 127,095,000 people, while Tokyo was an estimated 13,491,000 people.

Emperor Genshō
(r. 715-724)

Translated by Hiroko Manabe

Emperor of principle with a good disposition.
The first unmarried female emperor.

Circumstances of Enthronement

Emperor Genshō was the fifth female emperor. Known before enthronement as Princess Hidaka, she was born in Tenmu 9 (680) to the preceding Emperor Genmei and Prince Kusakabe, who died young. As a granddaughter of Emperor Tenmu and Emperor Jitō, as well as a granddaughter of Emperor Tenji, Genshō had an esteemed lineage. Her mother, the future Emperor Genmei, had two daughters and a son. Prince Obito, the son of her brother, Emperor Monmu, was next in line to ascend to the throne. However, when Prince Obito turned fifteen years old, he was of a frail disposition. Monmu's mother assumed that the prince, if enthroned, would surely need her help to administer state affairs until he matured. When Emperor Monmu passed away at the age of twenty-four, Monmu's mother, Emperor

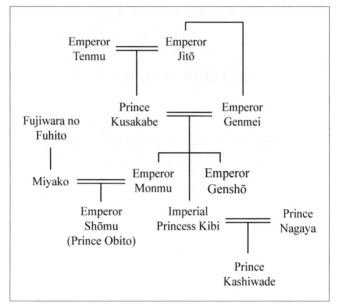

Lineage of Emperor Genshō

Genmei, succeeded as the intermediary emperor in place of Obito. Ultimately, however, prior to Prince Obito's coming of age, Genmei decided to transfer the throne to her own daughter, Princess Hidaka, who was thirty-six years old and unwed.

In the decree issued by Emperor Genmei at the time there was a passage as follows: "...in accordance with the rule, from henceforth, in perpetuity, [the throne shall pass to] my child. They shall receive it with certainty, favor, and without fail..." These ideas concerning the preservation of the

Emperor Genshō   *163*

imperial family line were influenced by Emperor Tenji.[59] When Prince Obito later became Emperor Shōmu, he quoted Genmei's passage in his proclamations. Prince Obito's mother was Miyako, daughter of Fujiwara no Fuhito, who was not a member of the imperial family. While there had previously been an emperor whose mother was not of the imperial line (Emperor Kōbun, formerly Prince Ōtomo, who was defeated in the Jinshin War), the Fujiwara desired to gain the advantage of having a Fujiwara family grandson become emperor.

The Fujiwara family's rise to prominence began with Kamatari. Kamatari overthrew the Soga (645), who had held the reigns of power, and handed over that power to the imperial family, thus forming a foundation for direct imperial rule. Under Emperor Genmei, Kamatari's son Fuhito assumed control of the government. Prince Obito was Fuhito's grandson. For this reason, as well as his capability, Emperor Genmei may have been concerned with making the young prince the next emperor. Whereupon, she conducted the celebration of his coming of age when he turned fifteen years

---

[59] Genmei was likely referring to precedents set by Emperor Jitō that harkened to Emperor Tenji's authority to justify a particular line of succession. See Herman Ooms, *Imperial Politics and Symbolics in Ancient Japan: The Tenmu Dynasty, 650-800* (Honolulu: University of Hawai'i Press, 2008), 25.

old, and, promising his future place as emperor, then transferred the throne to her daughter Princess Hidaka. Emperor Genmei was fifty-seven years old at the time. Princess Hidaka, on the other hand, was thirty-six years old. She would be able to fulfill the emperor's duties competently. In a statement at the time of her abdication, Emperor Genmei spoke very highly of Princess Hidaka as a woman of integrity. Princess Hidaka ascended to the throne and became the 44th Emperor Genshō, known by the title "Yamato Neko Taka Kiyotarashi Hime Tennō."

Shoku Nihongi described Hidaka as a serious-minded woman of principle. When she talked, she was always reasonable and compassionate. Although her record pales beside the other six female emperors, she accomplished a considerable number of undertakings during her nine-year reign.

Genshō's Reign

Emperor Genshō's enthronement ceremony was held on Reiki 1 (715).9.2. She appeared in the Imperial Council Hall and expressed her determination with dignity:

> I respectfully accept former Emperor Genmei's command to take the throne. I dare not decline nor recommend anyone else to succeed because I myself

want to bring peace and prosperity to this land.

The Left Capital Office (*sakyōshiki*) then presented the new emperor with a tortoise, regarded as an auspicious animal. She considered it as a gift from heaven, and declared:

> I will change the name of this period from Wadō to Reiki. The eighth year of Wadō will thus be the first year of Reiki.

The kanji for "Reiki 霊亀" are "spirit 霊" and "tortoise 亀." Then, according to custom, she issued proclamations of amnesty, conferment of court ranks, awards, special goods distributions, tax exemptions, and recognitions of meritorious services. Aside from these more conventional edicts, she also announced a lifetime tax exemption for certain people who were obedient children, good grandchildren, dutiful husbands, and devoted wives. They were told to hang plates of recognition at their front doors and at the entrances of their villages.

Three Era Name Changes

As stated above, with the accession of Emperor Genshō, the era name was changed from Wadō to Reiki. It was a common practice for a new emperor to announce such a change at their coronation. However, two years later, she

166

changed it again to Yōrō.[60] The third change to the Jinki era took place in the ninth month of the seventh year of Yōrō (723). The family of Sakyō no ki no ason presented a white tortoise to Emperor Genshō. She ordered court scholars to look through the books for references to white tortoises. Their research found that when a ruler was devoted to their parents, a dragon would appear from heaven, and a tortoise from the earth. Further, when a ruler governs their land fairly and virtuously, a divine tortoise would appear. The emperor appreciated this wonderful gift immensely, and changed the era name to Jinki (literally, "*kami* tortoise").

The most striking aspect of her reign is, much like Emperor Genmei, the unusually high number of imperial decrees she issued. Many of them were lengthy. These decrees demonstrate her strong will and profound understanding of contemporary circumstances.

Political and Economic Affairs

Genshō's frequent decrees addressed the government's measures for political and economic affairs. In the first proclamation, issued in the first year of Reiki (715), the emperor stated:

---

[60] Refer to Column 6 for the circumstances.

Emperor Genshō   *167*

The land will prosper and be peaceful only when the people's well-being is secured. They have to learn to save money. If men work hard in the field, and women at weaving, the family will be able to live comfortably in due time. If all the people are sensible and conduct themselves honorably, society needs no penalty or punishment, and they can live quietly.

In reality, they only grow rice plants in the marsh land without knowing there are other grains they can cultivate in the field. Consequently, when drought or flood hits the area, they lose all their crops. With no food stored, they go hungry. However, the government should not denounce them for ignorance or neglect. Rather, the provincial administrators should be blamed for not teaching and guiding them.

Make them plant both rice and wheat. Distribute the land in such a way so that each adult male works on two *tan* of field.[61] Millet is the best grain because it keeps for a long time in storage. Give this information to the farm workers and help them achieve the best

---

[61] 1 *tan* = 0.245 acres

outcome. Allot the other grains to them according to their abilities. If any want to pay taxes with millet in place of wheat, allow them to do so.

The statement reflects her thoughtful approach to the needs of the country and the people. Though we cannot determine to what extent Genshō's officials advised her in these matters, regardless, she promoted an extensive agenda and was firmly resolved to achieve prosperity for the land and the people. Several years later, in the seventh month of the sixth year of Yōrō (722), there was a drought and many crops failed. The government instructed the workers to plant late rice, buckwheat, barley, and wheat, and to stock them for the year of bad crop to come. People paid their taxes in three forms, taxes in kind, taxes in labor, and taxes in rice. For special country-wide celebrations, or in the case of mysterious celestial phenomena, taxes might be reduced. The poor and the aged were occasionally exempted.

The agricultural and local products for taxes in kind were delivered to the Heijō capital by carriers from the provinces. The government evaluated individual provincial administrators based on the conditions of the carriers, and poor performers were reprimanded. Relying on reports from the relevant cabinet officials, the emperor gave specific instructions for how to manage these matters. It may appear that Emperor Genshō's administration was stricter with officials than with

Emperor Genshō   *169*

the general public, but any violation of the law, whether by officials or others, was punished severely. On Yōrō 1 (717).4. 23, a decree was issued detailing penal regulations pertaining to monks and nuns. The offenses were classified in three categories, with each assigned its appropriate punishment.

The need for Genshō to issue such comprehensive edicts regarding the population's food production and farming techniques reflects the poverty experienced at the time. The well-known poem by Yamanoue no Okura, *Hinkyū mondō ka* ("Dialogue on Poverty"),[62] provides evidence as to how the masses lived. The poem was written in two parts. The first part asks a question and the second gives the answer in the form of a *tanka* (short poem).[63] Excerpts from the poem describe a farm worker drinking *kasuyuzake* (a watery drink made from the dregs of sake) and nibbling *katashio* (raw salt) "...on a night when it rains mixed with wind, on a night when it is windy mixed with rain." He has a fit of coughing and wipes his dirty nose, bragging, "I am the greatest in the world. Yes, I am..." It is so cold that he puts on a linen blanket. Still cold, he layers more clothes over it, saying:

---

[62] MYS 5.892, 5.893.

[63] *Tanka* 短歌 is a type of poetry composed in a 5-7-5-7-7 syllabic pattern.

I wonder how the poorer people are getting along on a night like this. Perhaps their old parents are hungry and shivering from the cold, and their children and wives are begging for food. How are they going to survive ?

His friend answers:

We were born in this world as human beings, but live in miserable conditions. We are so poor. Our robes are "not lined with cotton wool," and what is worse, they are worn to shreds. At night, we spread straw on the mud floor of our "tilted shabby little hut" and sleep on it, my parents at my head, my children and wife at my feet, covered with the tattered robes. The stove has not been used for a while. Cobwebs are hanging in the rice steamer, and my wife does not know how to steam rice any more. While we wail like night birds, the village chief comes to our bedside with a whip in his hand and demands that I pay the taxes. As a saying goes, he is here to "cut off a portion from the shortest end of the rope." What a hard life !

Then, he concludes his answer with a tanka:

though we may believe
this world of ours is harsh and
filled with pain,
we cannot take wing and fly
away - we are not birds

yo no naka o / ushi to yasashi to / omoedomo /
tobitachi kanetsu / tori ni shi araneba

[MYS 5.893]

Although Okura actually wrote this lengthy poem during the next emperor's reign, he was once a provincial administrator who saw and heard about farm workers' daily lives. He based this poem on those experiences, and thus gave commoners a voice.

Emperor Genshō was much concerned about the quality of life of her people. As stated, she undertook measures to improve agricultural output and, when necessary, exempted the poor from taxes. In Yōrō 3 (719), she initiated a loan system called *suiko* (the name being unrelated to Emperor Suiko),[64] and designated supervisors (*azechi*) to oversee the provincial administrators. By then, more and more provinces were being established. For example, the four districts in

---

[64] See column 5.

172

Kamifusa province, Heguri, Awa, Asahina, and Nagasa, were combined to make the new Awa province. Consequently, more administrators were appointed.

Column 5

The Loan System called "suiko"

There was a credit system before the establishment of the Taihō Code carried out with the goal of incentivizing agriculture and rescuing poor people. Loans were mainly conducted using rice, but also sometimes utilized millet, cash, or sake. Collateral included not only rice fields, but also houses, fabric, and even servants. These "public loans" (*suiko*) involved the provincial governments lending rice it collected as taxes in the spring and claiming its return at harvest time in the fall, with 5% (or sometimes 3%) interest added. However, with the passage of time, the debt collection in the fall became so strict that it turned to a kind of miscellaneous tax. The burden on farmers grew heavier, until they sold their allotments and fled to other provinces. This increased the vagrant population and ruined farmers' lives.

Emperor Genshō   *173*

In the section of the *Shoku Nihongi* on Emperor Genshō, we see many statements that she "did various things that had never been done before in Japan." For example, in the fourth month of the seventh year of Yōrō (723), a new law was enacted based on a report from the Great Council of State (*daijōkan*). Due to the increase in population, more rice fields were needed. The government encouraged farm workers to bring wasteland under cultivation. Under the new law, a man who reclaimed unused land could own it for three generations of his family. It also allowed a man who reclaimed a parcel of marshland to use it for his entire lifetime. Hence, it was called the "Law of Three Generations and One Generation" (*sanze isshin no hō*).

Around the same time, Fujiwara no Fuhito led the discussions over the updating of the Taihō Codes, debates that had been ongoing since the second year of Yōrō. However, with his passing two years later, talks on the matter came to a standstill.

There were conflicts in the Ezo area and with the Hayato people.[65] When the Hayato rose against the Heijō regime in the second year of Yōrō (718), Ootomo no Tabito was

---

[65] The Hayato 隼人, which literally means "falcon-people," were a group people in ancient Japan who lived in the southern region of Kyushu and often resisted Yamato rule.

174

appointed interim commander-in-chief and charged with the subjugation of the Hayato. As for foreign relations, the ties with Koma, Shiragi, and Kudara, established in the previous regime, continued without interruption. The government brought together 1, 779 people from Koma who had been living scattered across seven provinces and moved them to Musashi Province, creating the Koma district. Envoys were dispatched to China just as the previous reigns had done. In the eighth month of Reiki 2 (716), a group of envoys was sent to China on four ships. The leader of the group was Tajihi no Mahito agatanushi, who had assisted with the planning of the Heijō capital.

The Law of Priests and Nuns

Emperor Genshō placed great importance on Buddhism. On Reiki 2 (716). 5. 25, she issued a lengthy decree on temples, complaining that although a temple is a place of sanctity, many temples do not follow Buddhist law. While building shoddy structures, monks pretended as if they planned to build splendid ones, and made deceitfully earnest appeals to the authorities for more temple land and temple fields to line their pockets. Meanwhile, the temples were falling into decay, with dust covering the statues of worship and sutras exposed to the winds and rain. Given this offense to Buddhist teachings, Genshō planned to restore "declining

Emperor Genshō   *175*

Buddhist laws" and take the necessary measures, even if it meant seizing temples. She ordered that the provincial administrators were to have chief priests, monks, congregations, and benefactors submit inventories of their assets. In addition, even though there were temples in various provinces with pagoda halls, they had no residing priests or nuns. The decendants of benefactors were managing the land, and since no one was acting as priest to mediate, their disputes were endless. Genshō ordered for these problems to cease. Fujiwara no Muchimaro, the governor of Ōmi province at the time, was one of the court members who had warned the emperor that corruption in the temples would lead to the destruction of Buddhism.

Emperor Genshō also established clear policies on matters concerning religious figures. In a decree issued on Yōrō 1 (717). 4. 23, she condemned corrupt priests while dividing them into three categories: unqualified priests, who were common people entering the priesthood without any training or certification; priests who neglected their ascetic exercises and misled people on the streets by spreading false teachings; and priests who called on houses, where they gave sick people questionable remedies and took money for them.[66]

---

[66] Genshō alluded to the famous priest Gyōki in his youth as an example of this.

Genshō often spoke out strongly against the corrupt practices of Buddhist priests and temples and lobbied hard for the restoration of Buddhist teachings.

In an article from *Shoku Nihongi* dated Yōrō 4 (720). 5. 21, there is the following statement: "Prince Toneri was ordered by the emperor to take part in the compilation of the *Nihon shoki*. It was completed, and he presented thirty volumes of books and one volume of genealogical charts to the emperor." Prince Toneri, the chief editor of *Nihon shoki*, was Emperor Tenmu's fifth son. Emperor Tenmu initiated the compilation of this imperial history in 681, and, after myriad complications, the *Nihon shoki* was finished thirty-nine years later. Important contributions to Japanese history, both the compilations of the *Kojiki* and the *Nihon shoki* were completed during the reigns of female emperors, Emperor Genmei and Emperor Genshō respectively.

The Latter Days of Emperor Genshō's Reign

Emperor Genshō traveled often to Mino province as well as her Naniwa and Izumi residences. She also made a trip to Yoshino, which no emperor had visited since Emperor Jitō. Genshō often issued decrees concerning regulations on clothing. In one decree, issued in the second month of Yōrō 3 (719), she dictated that a kimono be put on with the right side of the kimono over the left. In the twelfth month (719),

Emperor Genshō
177

she standardized the style of women's clothing. Another initiative recorded in *Shoku Nihongi* was Genshō's creation of an official title for female doctors. She selected thirty intelligent women between fifteen and twenty-five years old and had them educated, teaching them obstetrics, gynecology, basic surgery, acupuncture, and moxibustion. After the training, they were tested, and, upon passing, received the official title. This was a remarkably progressive concept for the time.

In the second month of Jinki 1 (724), Emperor Genshō passed the throne to Crown Prince Obito. With the aforementioned appearance of a white tortoise, she was convinced that it was time. Her reign lasted nine years. *Shoku Nihongi* offers few accounts of her activities after abdication, but *Man'yōshū* includes five poems she wrote in those days. Here is one of them:

> when I journeyed along
> the foot-wearying mountains,
> the people of the mountains
> gave me this gift,
> it is this!

ashibikino / yama yukishi kaba / yamabito no /
ware ni e shimeshi / yamatsuto zo kore

[MYS 20.4293]

In seventh month of Tenpyō 8 (736), Retired Emperor Genshō fell ill, and the entire country prayed for her recovery. The prayers were answered, as she regained her health. From that point on, she lived with Emperor Shōmu at the palace. On Tenpyō 15 (743).5.5, Emperor Shōmu held the *gosechi no mai*, a celebratory dance for the emperor, at the imperial palace.[67] On that occasion Genshō composed the following poem:

in the country of Yamato
bestowed from the gods
looking down from below
how splendid it appears
when I see that dance!

bestowed by our emperor,
the living grandchild of the
heavenly gods,
we now can offer up

---

[67] The *gosechi no mai* 五節舞 was an elaborate event held by the emperor every year over a four-day period. Four or five girls performed court dances before the emperor each day in a different hall of the palace. Two girls were chosen from among the high rank courtiers' daughters while the others were daughters of provincial administrators.

Emperor Genshō   *179*

this splendid wine!

the reign of
our great sovereign
is tranquil and long:
now she partakes
of the splendid wine

sora mitsu / yamato no kuni wa / kami karashi /
tootoku arurashi/kono mai mireba

amatsu kami / mima no Mikoto no / torimochite /
kono toyomiki o / ima tatematsuru

yasumishishi / wa go ookimi wa / tairakeku /
nagaku imashite / toyomiki matsuru

[SNG, Tenpyō 15.5.5]

Also, at a court banquet on Tenpyō 19 (747).5.5, she stated,
"People used to wear the iris ornament in their hair for this
banquet, but these days nobody follows this custom any
longer. From this day forth, those without iris ornaments will
not be permitted to enter the palace [for the *gosechi*]."

Retired Emperor Genshō passed away at the age of sixty-
nine on Tenpyō 20 (748).4.21. On the twenty-eighth day of
the fourth month, she was cremated at the Sahoyama imperial

tomb, and later, in the second year of Tenpyō shōhō (750), her ashes were transferred to the Naho imperial tomb.

During Emperor Genshō's reign, Fujiwara no Fuhito (the father of her sister-in-law, Miyako, wife of Emperor Monmu) and the other officials supported her faithfully. Fuhito's four sons, Muchimaro, Fusasaki, Umakai and Maro, also held important offices in the government. Their prominence and the strategic placement of other Fujiwara family members facilitated the increased power of the Fujiwara family at the imperial court. After Fuhito's passing in the eighth month of Yōrō 4 (720), Prince Nagaya took hold of power as Minister of the Right. Prince Nagaya was Emperor Tenmu's grandson and Prince Takechi's first son. His mother was Emperor Tenji's daughter, Princess Minabe. Prince Nagaya therefore came from noble stock, and this helped advance his position. He later was appointed to the influential role of Minister of the Left at the time of Emperor Shōmu's enthronement. Prince Nagaya was likely resentful about the pronounced influence of the Fujiwara. In the second month Jinki 1 (724), Emperor Shōmu conferred a title, the Grand Consort (*daibunin*), on his mother, Fujiwara no Miyako. Citing restrictions in the *ritsuryō* codes, Prince Nagaya opposed such a conferment on someone not of imperial blood, and the emperor instead had to confer a lesser title. Prince Nagaya's antipathy toward the Fujiwara would later culminate in the Prince Nagaya Incident.

Column 6

The "Augury of Beauty"? How the era name "Yōrō" came about

In the ninth month of the first year of Reiki (715-717), the emperor visited Mino province. She stayed at the temporary palace in Fuwa and went to Mt. Tado (Mt. Yōrō) in the village of Taki, where she saw a beautiful spring. After returning to the Heijō capital (Nara), she issued a rescript in the eleventh month that stated: When I washed my face and hands in the beautiful spring, they became smooth, and when I washed areas that were sore, the pain was immediately relieved. And I heard that when one drank this water or bathed in it, one's white hair turned black, and hair grew on a bald head. Eyes that could not see regained sight, and prolonged illnesses were cured. According to ancient Chinese texts, it is written that this kind of clear spring can rejuvenate old age. The spirit of this water is an auspicious sign. As someone who is no one special, I cannot ignore such a propitious omen.

She then changed the era name Reiki to Yōrō ("nurturing the old").

Emperor Kōken
(r. 749-758)

Translated by Paula R. Curtis

The first female crown prince,
single all her life and
a deep believer in Buddhism.

Emperor Kōken, the seventh female emperor, was the forty-sixth ruler of Japan. Under Emperor Shōmu, she was bestowed the title of imperial princess,[68] and her personal name was Princess Abe. Kōken's mother was Empress Kōmyō and her father Fujiwara no Fuhito. In Jinki 4 (727).9, Emperor Shōmu sired an imperial prince, Motoi, and only a month later, Motoi was made crown prince. However, Motoi was sickly from birth, and despite fervent prayers on his

---

[68] *Naishinnō* 内親王, translated here as "imperial princess," is a designation given by imperial command to a royal descendent officially recognizing her as a member of the royal house. Unlike Western interpretations of terms such as "imperial princess," this title does not suggest the recipient is necessarily the direct offspring of the emperor.

Emperor Kōken   *183*

behalf, in the ninth month of 728, he died at only two years old. The title of crown prince (*kōtaishi*) went unused for ten years before Imperial Princess Abe succeeded to the position in Tenpyō 10 (738). 1. As the first woman with this title, Kōken assisted her father, the emperor, for twelve years. In the first year of the Tenpyō shōhō period (749), Emperor Shōmu abdicated and Kōken was enthroned.

Emperor Kōken took the tonsure later in life, so after her death, unlike other emperors, she did not have a posthumous Buddhist name and was called Emperor Hōji Shōtoku Kōken. She was also called Emperor Takano and Takano hime no mikoto.

Emperor Shōmu

As crown prince under Emperor Shōmu, Emperor Kōken was actively involved in his reign. Emperor Shōmu ruled for twenty-five years (724-749), a length second only to Emperor Suiko's thirty-six-year reign from 592 to 628.

The Construction of the Daibutsu

The magnificent Nara Daibutsu (Great Buddha), now an UNESCO World Heritage Site in the city of Nara, received its last major repairs during the Shōwa period (1926-1989). Today, enshrined in the Great Buddha Hall (*Daibutsuden*) of

184

Tōdaiji Temple, it commands the attention of domestic and foreign sightseers as effortlessly as it did in the past. Although the Daibutsu was considered a rallying point for Nara Buddhism,[69] a multitude of political and religious circumstances laid the groundwork for the Daibutsu's creation. Work on the Daibutsu began under Emperor Shōmu's rule.

Emperor Shōmu was born in Taihō 1 (701) to Emperor Monmu and Fujiwara no Miyako. He became crown prince at age fourteen, and married Fujiwara no Fuhito's daughter. Shōmu was enthroned ten years later, becoming emperor at age twenty-four. When Shōmu officially made Fuhito's daughter Kōmyō his empress, it was the first time someone not of the imperial line had been conferred that position. This appointment was an immense honor for the Fujiwara family, who were vying for political supremacy at court. In Jinki 4 (727), Prince Motoi, who was a potential candidate for

---

[69] Broadly speaking, the term "Nara Buddhism" refers to a period in the eighth century in which Buddhist practice and scholasticism flourished, particularly due to state sponsorship of six schools of Buddhism (Hossō, Jojitsu, Kegon, Kusha, Ritsu, Sanron). The court patronized a variety of Buddhist literary, artistic, and architectural projects, in part with the goal of using Buddhism to help centralize state authority and establish the emperor as a powerful protector of Buddhist law. To this end, the construction of the Daibutsu was an important symbol.

Emperor Kōken   *185*

emperor, was born. Although he was made crown prince only a month after his birth, he died of illness the following year. Meanwhile, the consort Agatainukai no Hirotoji gave birth to the imperial prince Asaka, complicating matters of succession. However, Asaka also died of illness, which was fortunate for the Fujiwara family.

Shortly after Shōmu's enthronement, the Prince Nagaya Incident occurred. As mentioned in the previous chapter, around this time, Prince Nagaya was gradually distinguishing himself at court and had ascended to the position of Minister of the Left, which made Emperor Shōmu apprehensive. Prince Nagaya would later become subject to a scheme of the Fujiwara family. He was falsely charged with learning black magic and attempting to overthrow the country, for which he was forced to commit suicide. This conflict had a variety of political ramifications. Imperial Princess Kibi was convicted and killed along with Nagaya, which was likely difficult on her only sister, Retired Emperor Genshō.

After this incident, Emperor Shōmu continued to govern while receiving advice from Genshō, and with Kōmyō officially becoming his empress, the situation appeared to have stabilized. However, during the Tenpyō period (729-749), the country was plagued with repeated disasters and mysterious natural phenomena. Plagues spread in various provinces, and whenever drought struck the land, the emperor stated that it was "because of his own lack of virtue" that such misfortunes were happening. In order to regain heavenly favor, he gave offerings and prayers to the gods, performed sutra chanting at temples, made numerous people take the tonsure, and granted pardons, but to no effect. The coup de grâce was an alarming situation in Tenpyō 9 (737). Starting with four Fujiwara siblings (Muchimaro, Fusasaki, Umakai, and Maro) who had been central figures in the court government, many high-ranking officials died one after another within the span of half a year, the result of a widespread smallpox outbreak. Emperor Shōmu was deeply dismayed.

Natural disasters also continued to occur in succession. According to the *Shoku Nihongi*, earthquakes happened every day in the first half of the fifth month of Tenpyō 17 (745). Events such as earthquakes and solar eclipses had occurred frequently before, but, in this period, there were a conspicuously large number of ominous reports related to the stars. Given these tumultuous circumstances, the emperor, who was already a deep believer in Buddhism, turned to the Buddhist faith to placate the unstable environment. The emperor spread knowledge of the Golden Light Sutra in various provinces, ordered people in each province to copy the Lotus Sutra, and had them build seven-story pagodas. He issued an imperial decree for priests and nuns to establish state-sponsored provincial temples, commissioned the Daibutsu at Tōdaiji, and generally fostered a sense that the

Emperor Kōken   *187*

realm was being protected by devotion to Buddhist religious discipline. Over the course of ten years, the enormous Daibutsu (a representation of the Vairocana Buddha) continued to be built in the Heijō capital, known today as Nara.

The emperor's decision to build the Daibutsu purportedly occurred in Tenpyō 12 (740), when he worshipped before the Vairocana Buddha at the temple Chishikidera in Kawachi province. Prayers for the Daibutsu's completion were done in Tenpyō 15 (743), but despite the immense efforts of the laborers who began the metal casting process, by 747, the Daibutsu was still largely unfinished. In the second month of Tenpyō 21 (749), just when the emperor was troubled by an anonymous letter dropped on the street near the imperial court,[70] gold discovered in Mutsu was presented to the court. The emperor was pleased to have obtained gold that could be used to gild the surface of the Daibutsu. Immediately, Shōmu made an imperial visit to Tōdaiji Temple, and, facing north, sat near the Buddha image. In an edict presented there, he called himself the "Servant of the Three Treasures of Buddhism [the Buddha, the teachings of Buddhism, the

---

[70] On this subject, the *Shoku Nihongi* reports only that anonymous writings critical of the court were found, and an edict was issued for this activity to cease.

188

Buddhist community]" and expressed his gratitude to the deities. Empress Kōmyō and Crown Prince Abe were also in attendance. This was the first day of the fourth month, and on the fourteenth day, the emperor yet again went to Tōdaiji. It was also during this period that Emperor Shōmu's health began to fail; even more tirelessly committed to the Buddhist faith, he made 1, 000 people become monks, granted amnesties, and donated to the five temples of Daianji, Yakushiji, Gankōji, Kōfukuji, and Tōdaiji. Shōmu took up residence in Yakushiji Temple in the fifth month of Tenpyō shōhō 1 (749), just before his abdication in the seventh month. Written prayers of various temples record the tonsured name "Retired Emperor Shami shōman,"[71] reflecting Shōmu's deep commitment to Buddhism in his later years.

Moving the Capital

Traditionally, it has been thought that from the time of Emperor Genmei's transfer of the capital to Heijō in Wadō 3 (710) until Emperor Kanmu's transfer of the capital to Nagaoka in Enryaku 3 (784) the capital was located in Nara. In reality, Emperor Shōmu frequently moved the capital.

---

[71] The label *shami* 沙弥 was used to denote a novice monk in Buddhist practice.

Emperor Kōken

The first move began with the emperor's journey in Tenpyō 12 (740).10, when Shōmu stated "I have been thinking for a little while that I will go to the east," referring to provinces to the east of Ise and Mino. Shōmu departed on the twenty-ninth day of the tenth month, arriving first in Iga province, and, continuing to travel, stayed in temporary residences in various locations such as Ise, Mino, and Ōmi. As his journey continued, he occasionally enjoyed excursions such as for hunting. On the fifteenth day of the twelfth month, the emperor entered the Mikanohara villa in the Sagara district of Yamashiro province, reported that he wished to make this location the new Ooyamato Kuni no miya capital, and ordered the commencement of construction. Retired Emperor Genshō and Empress Kōmyō arrived later. The following year, in the first month of Tenpyō 13 (741), the annual New Year's greetings from retainers were received at Kuni no miya.[72]

The Mikanohara villa, previously called Okada villa, was a residence where both emperors Genmei and Genshō often rested; this was one reason the establishment of a new capital began there. Quite different from the Heijō capital, the lands

---

[72] The annual New Year's greetings, or *chōga* 朝賀, was a ceremony occurring on New Year's Day in which retainers below the rank of crown prince called upon the court to provide their well-wishes to the emperor and empress for the new year.

of Kuni no miya were surrounded on three sides by mountains and narrow. The construction was therefore an immense undertaking and the manual labor necessary was immeasurable. Though the Imperial Council Hall of the imperial palace and its various cloisters were dismantled and brought to Kuni no miya, after two years, the transfer of the capital was still not complete. Furthermore, in autumn of 742, Emperor Shōmu ordered that a villa be constructed in the village of Shigaraki in Kōka (present day Shiga prefecture), and subsequently left for an eight-day stay at Shigaraki no miya before he returned to Kuni no miya. As the end of the year approached, Shōmu once again left for Shigaraki no miya. But when the new year arrived, on the third day of the first month of Tenpyō 15 (743), the emperor received palace visits at Kuni no miya. In the fourth month, he traveled again to Shigaraki no miya. On the fifth day of the fifth month, a banquet was thrown at Kuni no miya, where Crown Prince Abe (the later Emperor Kōken) danced a *gosechi* dance. Given that *gosechi* dances were done by women, it was unprecedented for a crown prince to give such a performance. Retired Emperor Genshō was in attendance and composed the following poem:

> in the country of Yamato
> bestowed from the gods
> looking down from below
> how splendid it appears

when I see that dance!

sora mitsu / yamato no kuni wa / kami karashi /
tootoku arurashi / kono mai mireba

[SNG, Tenpyō 15.5.5]

Seeing this beautiful dance, Genshō gave a tribute to Yamato
(Japan), saying that Yamato was esteemed because it was the
land of the gods (*kami*).

During that year, Emperor Shōmu traveled twice more to
the Shigaraki no miya. It took four years before the emperor
finally terminated construction on Kuni no miya, and the
expenses incurred during that period were immense. At the
same time, construction had also been going on at Shigaraki
no miya, so work on Kuni no miya had to be stopped for
financial reasons.

In the first month of Tenpyō 16 (744), Emperor Shōmu
went to Naniwa no miya. There, he gathered all the court
officials and asked them whether they thought Kuni no miya
or Naniwa no miya should be the capital. In response, twenty-
four people above fifth rank and one hundred and fifty-seven
people below sixth rank said Kuni no miya was the better
choice, while twenty-three people above fifth rank and one
hundred and thirty people below sixth rank said Naniwa was
better. Additionally, surveyors went into local markets and
did what might today be called "on-the-street interviews,"

and, other than a handful of people who favored Naniwa or the Heijō capital, everyone chose Kuni no miya. With this, Kuni no miya was selected as the new site of the capital. It is unusual that the emperor took into account the opinions of people of various social statuses.

However, this decision did not mean that the matter of the capital was settled. On the eleventh day of the first month, Emperor Shōmu once again left for Naniwa no miya. Supervising government affairs from Naniwa, he ordered for the imperial bells, imperial seals, and throne (objects used during everyday governance) to be brought there and, in the second month, he called his court officials to serve at his location. In the meanwhile, the emperor appointed high-ranking palace caretakers to manage the Heijō capital and Kuni no miya. On the twenty-sixth day of the second month, Shōmu issued an imperial order stating: "I have decided that the capital will be Naniwa from now on." During this time, the emperor also spent a number of days at Izumi no miya (another imperial villa) and Shigaraki no miya. In the fourth month, construction at Shigaraki began. Emperor Shōmu returned to Naniwa no miya in the tenth month, but in the first month of the following year, Tenpyō 17 (745), he suddenly decided to relocate the capital to Shigaraki no miya. This was the aforementioned year in which successive calamities took place. Perhaps because of these misfortunes, Emperor Shōmu returned to Kuni no miya, had sutras read at temples in Heijō for the protection of the land, and, on the eleventh day of the fifth month, returned via imperial transport to the Heijō capital.

Although it appeared as if Emperor Shōmu might finally settle down, his habit of moving locations continued. Within the same year, he yet again went to Naniwa and returned to the Heijō capital on the fifth day of the ninth month. From this point forward, a government wholly devoted to Buddhism began to take shape. The emperor moved his residence to Yakushiji Temple, and on the second day of the seventh month of Tenpyō shōhō 1 (749), Crown Prince Abe was enthroned. The emperor's tendency to move the capital no doubt had a significant impact on everyday political operations. In Tenpyō shōhō 8 (756), seven years after Shōmu's abdication, he died. The belongings he left behind, gorgeous examples of Tenpyō culture, are now preserved as imperial treasures at the Shōsōin Repository in Nara.

The Era of Emperor Kōken

The first female crown prince

Emperor Kōken became Emperor Shōmu's crown prince in Tenpyō 10 (738) at the age of seventeen. She held the rank of crown prince for twelve years, providing her with intimate knowledge of Emperor Shōmu's reign. Unlike the female emperors before her, Kōken saw with her own eyes all of the land she would soon rule.

Early on, as Imperial Princess Abe, Kōken's position as crown prince was complicated by various political machinations and events. As previously mentioned, one was the death of Prince Motoi in 728 and the birth of Prince Asaka in the same year to one of Emperor Shōmu's consorts, Agatainukai no Hirotoji. If Prince Asaka, now eleven years old, continued to live, he could become a crown prince not born of a Fujiwara mother, impairing the lofty political ambitions of the Fujiwara family. And after the deaths of the four Fujiwara brothers, the central figure of the Fujiwara family became Muchimaro's eldest son Toyonari, but he was not considered capable of carrying out their political objectives. Since Emperor Shōmu and Empress Kōmyō did not produce a second prince as a potential imperial successor, there was no better prospect to name crown prince and inherit the throne than the royal couple's own daughter, Imperial Princess Abe, who was herself of Fujiwara heritage. With this, for the first and last time in Japan's history, a female crown prince was born. After Crown Prince Abe was enthroned, Prince Asaka became crown prince. However, Asaka died of illness shortly thereafter in 744, at only sixteen years of age. There are a number of poems left in the *Man'yōshū* on this subject by Ootomo no Yakamochi, who was close to the prince.

Tachibana no Moroe (684-757) was one person who wielded power in the government on behalf of the Fujiwara family. Moroe, also called Prince Katsuragi, was the son of Prince Minu and Agatainukai no Michiyo. Considered an imperial family member, he took his mother's name, Tachibana, and participated in government affairs as Tachibana no Moroe. Michiyo later remarried Fujiwara no Fuhito, so Moroe became a stepbrother to both Emperor Shōmu's mother, Miyako, and Empress Kōmyō. Furthermore, Moroe gradually extended his influence and acquired the powerful office of the Minister of the Left. His son Naramaro would later incite a rebellion against Emperor Kōken. Amidst this turbulent political environment, Crown Prince Abe received the throne from her father, Emperor Shōmu, and ascended to the role of emperor in 749.

Kōken as Emperor

With the exception of Emperor Genshō, previous female emperors had been empresses of reigning emperors, and fulfilled an intermediary role, holding the position for a child successor until their maturity. Emperor Genshō was single and not an empress, but as emperor, she held the place for her nephew Obito (Emperor Shōmu) until his adulthood. Emperor Kōken's situation was slightly different, as she was enthroned through the traditional custom of appointment to crown prince. Kōken's rise to power was unlike any other in that she, as a woman, was made emperor in order to preserve the imperial line in the same manner that a man would have been.

Emperor Kōken's ascension was celebrated on Tenpyō kanpō 1. 7. 2 (749). As was customary upon a new enthronement, the era name was changed to the first year of the Tenpyō shōhō period. As a result, 749 was an unusual year for historical dating: from the first month to fourth month was Tenpyō 21, from the fourth month to the seventh month was Tenpyō kanpō 1, and from the seventh month it was Tenpyō shōhō 1. The enthronement celebration occurred at the Imperial Council Hall in the palace, but an article in the *Shoku Nihongi* states that in the following year, the New Year's greetings of the court were received in the audience hall of the Heijō Palace, after which Kōken returned to the Oogo'ori palace, so it is surmised that at the time of her enthronement, the emperor was regularly residing at Oogo'ori. The location of the Oogo'ori Palace is not clear, but one theory is that it is near Yamato ko'oriyama in northern Nara.[73] Kōken may have stayed there because at the time, the Heijō Palace was under repair. As a result, it is possible that,

---

[73] Evidence also suggests the possibility of Oogo'ori palace having existed in Naniwa, placing it in Osaka rather than Nara.

Emperor Kōken   *197*

along with the enthronement performed in the eleventh month, the First Offering Harvest Rites (*daijōsai*)[74] occurred in the new palace's pleasure gardens at Ko'oriyama. This was unprecedented, and was said to have occurred specifically because the emperor was a woman. Emperor Kōken's reign began under these exceptional circumstances. Kōken's government operations were organized through the vigorous assistance of the Empress Dowager Kōmyō and Fujiwara no Nakamaro (706-764), the director of the Empress Dowager's administrative office (*shibi chūdai*).[75]

In the *Shoku Nihongi,* the articles on Emperor Kōken differ significantly in style and content compared to those on emperors Genmei and Genshō. In the case of the latter two emperors, imperial decrees were issued copiously and in quite a bit of detail, whereas for Kōken, there are few such entries. There are a number of articles about investiture, amnesty, or

---

[74] The *daijōsai*大嘗祭, or First Offering Harvest Rites, the first rite performed upon enthronement, is one of the most important large-scale court ceremonies. The new emperor makes an offering of the first of the harvested grains to the *kami* to ensure the longevity and prosperity of the realm.

[75] The *shibi chūdai* 紫微中台 was an extrastatutory office established in 749 tasked primarily with handling Kōmyō's affairs. Its members were all high-ranking officials, and Nakamaro's assumption of the position of director accorded him considerable political influence.

198

other personnel affairs, but, other than that, the most notable writings relate to Kōken's dispatching of envoys to T'ang China, relations with Shiragi, controlling misgovernment by provincial administrators, or proclamations of the Yōrō Codes. In the first half of these articles, there are many related to Buddhism.

Very much her father's daughter, Kōken held a deep faith in Buddhism. In this vein, she continued the previous period's grand enterprise of constructing the Daibutsu. The eye-opening ceremony of the Daibutsu was successfully completed on Tenpyō shōhō 4 (752).4.9.[76] The emperor was accompanied to the site by all her officials and a grand Buddhist mass was held. The eye-opening ceremony, unable to be accomplished during Emperor Shōmu's reign, was at last conducted with the echoing voices of 10, 000 monks chanting sutras and the visiting priest Bodhisena as officiator. They played *gagaku* music and other such court dance and music was also performed by various attendants. The ceremony was said to be so glorious that it could not be captured in words, and historical texts stated that "there had never been such a magnificent Buddhist assembly since Buddhism was first transmitted to the East." The grandest ceremony of the age, Emperor Kōken was the leading figure

---

[76] See footnote 48.

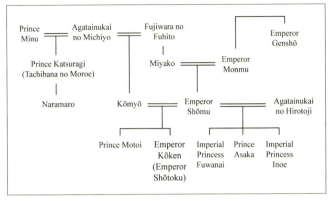

Lineage of Emperor Koken

at the ceremony. Retired Emperor Shōmu, going by the name Shami Shōman (his tonsured name), was also in attendance to pray, along with Empress Dowager Kōmyō. Innumerable people were involved in the ceremony's undertaking. With this, the Vairocana Buddha at last appeared in the Heijō capital to protect the land, just as Emperor Shōmu had prayed for.

Emperor Kōken had been raised with a deeply Buddhist heart, and her reign continued to be an age of Buddhist prosperity. Beginning with Tōdaiji Temple, Kōken frequently had provincial temples recite sacred books and copy sutras, produce Buddhist statues, and tonsure new priests. In Tenpyō shōhō 6 (754). 1. 16, the vice-envoy to China, Ootomo no Sukune Komaro, completed his duties and safely returned to Japan, bringing with him the T'ang priest Jianzhen (688-

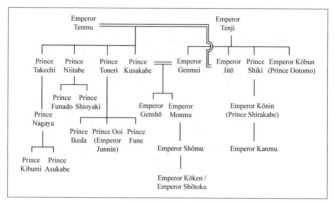

Lineage of Emperor Tenmu and Emperor Tenji

763). Jianzhen was first invited to Japan in 742 under Shōmu's rule, but the voyage failed at least seven times due to inclement weather and government interference. By the time it finally succeeded, Jianzhen was blind. The court, however, treated Jianzhen respectfully; he was allowed to found Tōshōdaiji Temple in 759, and, after that, spent the rest of his life there. Under the patronage of both emperors Shōmu and Kōken, Jianzhen propagated his teachings to various priests and ordained Emperor Shōmu and Empress Dowager Kōmyō. Today, the portrait statue of Jianzhen is a secret figure (normally withheld from the public) at Tōshōdaiji Temple. The doors to container housing the figure are opened only once a year, in June, for public viewing. In the Tokugawa period, the poet Matsuo Bashō (1644-1694) prayed at the temple and composed a haiku, now engraved on a stone

Emperor Kōken   *201*

monument there:

> with a new leaf
> I would like to wipe away
> the drops from Jianzhen's eyes

aoba shite / onme no shizuku / nuguwa baya

The sacred texts essential to the study of Buddhism at the time, such as the Lotus Sutra, Avatamska Sutra (*kegon-kyō*), Human King Sutra (*ninnogyō*), Sovereign Kings of the Golden Light Sutra (*konkōmyō saishōō-kyō*), and Brahmajala Sutra (*bonmō-kyō*) had considerable theoretical discrepancies and unfathomably complex worldviews. Despite their difficult content, Emperor Kōken was a dedicated devotee to Buddhist study. Not long after the great success of the Daibutsu's completion, Kōken became surrounded by sickness and death, and, for the devout emperor, her greatest emotional and moral support system was Buddhism. Her grandmother, Grand Empress Dowager Miyako, Emperor Shōmu, and Empress Dowager Kōmyō all suffered afflictions. Each time, Emperor Kōken, having no leisure for respite as she tended to them, sought personal comfort in her faith. Especially when her father Emperor Shōmu became ill at Naniwa, she spent as much as four months away from the capital attending to him. After the emperor's death, she mourned for more than a year, and on the anniversary of his death, she diligently held a proper Buddhist memorial. Throughout the nine years of Emperor Kōken's reign, she continued to maintain a profound devotion to Buddhist practice.

The Rebellion of Tachibana no Naramaro

Meanwhile, unrest surrounding Emperor Kōken's reign increased. Retired Emperor Shōmu willed the vacant position of crown prince to Prince Funado and died soon after. Funado was the child of Prince Niitabe, an imperial prince and son of Emperor Tenmu. Emperor Tenmu fathered ten imperial princes, so there were many grandchildren who also became princes, and there were other princes descended from Emperor Tenji's line, too. Many of them had reached a suitable age for succession, so choosing from among them was a difficult task. Emperor Kōken was single and had no heir, a problem that had vexed Emperor Shōmu. By establishing Prince Funado as crown prince, Shōmu assured the succession of the next reign.

However, Crown Prince Funado acted uncouthly while in mourning for Emperor Shōmu and his title was immediately deposed.[77] So Emperor Kōken again had to decide the next crown prince. From among her close associates, Fujiwara no Toyonari and Fujiwara no Nagate recommended Prince Funado's older brother Prince Shioyaki, and Bunya no Chinu and Ootomo no Komaru recommended the son of the Imperial Prince Toneri, Prince Ikeda. However, only Nakamaro said it should be "as the emperor wills it," and the emperor decided on Prince Ooi. Fujiwara no Nakamaro, the emperor's cousin, played a major role in this decision. Compared to his brother Toyonari, the Minister of the Right, Nakamaro was a shrewd political operator; for Emperor Kōken, who had lost her father and had no male siblings or children, Nakamaro was a trustworthy friend and adviser.

There were also political entities surreptitiously attempting to overthrow the government at the time. This conspiracy was spearheaded by Tachibana no Naramaro. Being the son of Moroe, Naramaro acquired a high rank appropriate to his birthright. At some point, he began to conspire with the discontented princes of the court, and rumors of their plans to overthrow the throne reached the ears of the emperor. Warnings regarding these plans had previously been reported a number of times, but because of Empress Dowager

---

[77] Prince Funado was deposed for engaging in sexual relations during a period of mourning for the former emperor. See Gary P. Leupp, *Male Colors: The Construction of Homosexuality in Tokugawa Japan* (Berkeley: University of California Press, 1995), 23.

Kōmyō's intervention, they never came to fruition. However, in Tenpyō hōji 1 (757), a decisive incident took place. A flurry of rumors reported that Naramaro's conspirators planned to stockpile weapons and encircle the emperor's temporary residence in Tamura, murder Nakamaro, and depose the crown prince. They would capture the palace of the Empress Dowager, seize the imperial bell and seal, dethrone the emperor, and choose a new emperor from among the four princes (Shioyaki, Asuka, Kibun, and Funado). The ringleaders of this incident, Naramaro, Ootomo no Komaro, Prince Shioyaki, Prince Asuka, and Prince Kibun (the grandson of Prince Takeichi) were caught and punished, ending the rebellion before it took place. For Emperor Kōken, it was a career-defining incident. Naramaro's excuse was that the building of the Daibutsu was a huge expense that had been a burden on the people. Empress Dowager Kōmyō is said to have lamented "Why, even though you are all my nephews, would you do this... ?"

Likely as a result of this incident, the imperial edicts that followed focused on the political administration of the upper levels of court. In Tenpyō hōji 2 (758), Emperor Kōken passed the throne to the crown prince, Prince Ooi. She was likely in a state of utter exhaustion from her duties as emperor and wanted to devote herself to nursing her sick mother, the Empress Dowager Kōmyō.

During Emperor Kōken's reign, the realm appeared

Emperor Kōken

peaceful, but that was merely the exterior, masking a turbulent political underbelly. The recently completed Daibutsu looked out over the Heijō capital standing guard over the people, but even that figure was mired in a variety of conflicts. It was Kōken's fate that she endured many burdens that the female emperors before her had not. Furthermore, even after abdication, she was involved in politics as the retired emperor, and eventually ascended the throne a second time.

There is one poem written by Emperor Kōken included in the *Man'yōshū*. According to the headnote of the poem, when the emperor went with Empress Dowager Kōmyō to the residences of Nakamaro, she had an attendant carry a colorful Eleorchis flower (swamp orchid) as a gift to him. Kōken wrote this to accompany it:

> in this village
> is there always frost?
> in the summer fields
> I saw the grasses
> tinged with autumn

kono sato wa / tsugite shimo ya oku / natsu no no ni /
wa ga mishi kusa wa / momiji tari keri

[MYS 19.4268]

As we shall see in the next chapter, Nakamaro was a close confidante of Emperor Kōken with intimate ties to the imperial family.

Emperor Kōken's filial duties to Empress Dowager Kōmyō were a central factor in her decision to transfer the throne, and also speak to the strength of Empress Dowager Kōmyō. As Emperor Shōmu's empress, Kōmyō supported Kōken, and after the death of Shōmu, she not only helped her daughter, the emperor, but achieved great things in politics. The influence of Kōmyō's personal character on Kōken is conveyed in articles written in *Shoku Nihongi,* which state Kōmyō was "wise from a young age," "elegant and devoted to Buddhism," and "a benevolent person who dedicated herself to the aid of others." Kōken also had great pride in being the daughter of Fujiwara no Fuhito. Kōmyō's devout, selfless, and strong character undoubtedly influenced those same traits in her daughter Kōken as much as Shōmu's guidance had during his rule.

Emperor Shōtoku

(r. 764-770)

Translated by Paula R. Curtis

The female emperor who appointed
Dōkyō, the monk who consoled
her in her grief and loneliness.
A tonsured emperor who governed
with a strong force of will
during times of personal turmoil.

Emperor Shōtoku, the eighth female emperor, was Emperor Kōken, who reascended the throne under a new name. After Emperor Kōken's abdication, the crown prince, Prince Ooi, became Emperor Junnin on the first day of the eighth month of Tenpyō hōji 2 (758). The forty-seventh emperor, Junnin, was young, only twenty-five years old. Furthermore, he had become crown prince suddenly. Unlike Kōken, who served as crown prince for twelve years before becoming emperor, Junnin occupied the position for less than a year before he inherited the throne. Emperor Kōken, who then became the retired emperor, was still in a position to guide politics. But the true mover and shaker in the political scene of the time was Fujiwara no Nakamaro, who continued his influence from the previous reign.

Nakamaro's Influence and Rebellion

Fujiwara no Nakamaro, as the second son of the influential Muchimaro, rose steadily in rank and established a strong presence in court. In Emperor Shōmu's time, Nakamaro was deeply trusted, and after the emperor's death, Nakamaro and Empress Dowager Kōmyō stood at the center of the political world as supporters of Emperor Kōken. At Nakamaro's suggestion, Prince Ooi married Awata no Morone, the widow of Nakamaro's eldest son Mayori, and lived in Nakamaro's residence. When the Heijō Palace was under repair, Emperor Kōken also lived in Nakamaro's residence in Tamura. Nakamaro's close position to the imperial family was therefore both well-recognized and assured. Nakamaro renamed the Empress Dowager's administrative office using a Chinese-style name, the *shibi chūdai*,[78] and became its director, which was equal in status to that of a cabinet minister. With this position, he was able to gain the trust of Empress Dowager Kōmyō. The aforementioned Tachibana no Naramaro had rebelled, in part,

---

[78] See footnote 75.

Emperor Shōtoku   *209*

against this kind of autocracy, but Nakamaro's influence was able to flourish with Naramaro eliminated. Before long, Nakamaro became Minister of the Right, and Emperor Junnin praised his unfailing loyalty. In the eighth month of Tenpyō hōji 2 (758), the emperor granted him the additional moniker "*emi* 恵美" to the Fujiwara name, taking the characters from the phrase "virtuousness (*bitoku* 美徳) that greatly invites blessings (*megumi* 恵み)." He also allowed Nakamaro to call himself "*oshikatsu* 押勝" from the phrase "he who subjugated those who cause outrages, won (*kachi* 勝ち) against formidable enemies, and suppressed (*oshishizumeta* 押し静めた) disturbances." These characters became the name "Emi no Oshikatsu 恵美押勝." Nakamaro was also granted farmland and a house stipend for his meritorious service. A person receiving so many honors as a retainer had seldom occurred since Emperor Tenji conferred the highest cap rank, *taishokkan*, to Nakamaro's grandfather. Prior to this, at the time of Emperor Kōken's abdication and Emperor Junnin's enthronement, Nakamaro was a model retainer, and received the honorary titles of *Jōdai Hōji Shōtoku Kōken kōtei* and *Chūdai Tenpyō ōshin ninshō kōtaigō*[79] from the retired emperor and Empress Dowager Kōmyō respectively. These titles, influenced by the names of Chinese constellations, also demonstrate Nakamaro's interest in China.

In the sixth month of Tenpyō hōji (760), around the time Empress Dowager Kōmyō died, the situation surrounding

Nakamaro (now Emi Oshikatsu) became unstable. As the Great Council of State, Nakamaro had full authority over the highest ranked retainers, and his sons, too, were given high rank and positions. Nakamaro administered government affairs as he desired, and though few conflicts were evident, beneath the surface, tensions brewed. One issue was the friction between Emperor Junnin and Retired Emperor Kōken.

In Hōji 3 (759), because of repairs to the Heijō palace, Emperor Junnin traveled to the Hora villa in Ōmi, and intended to make it the northern capital. Both he and Kōken stayed at the Hora villa for a short while, and during that time, Dōkyō (700-772) nursed her when she became ill. Emperor Junnin, seeing that the two of them were gradually becoming closer, advised against it a number of times, but this was at Nakamaro's suggestion. Having returned to the Heijō Palace in the fifth month of 762, Retired Emperor Kōken gathered all of the officials together on the third day of the sixth month and gave the following decree:

---

[79] In ancient China, *jōdai* 上台 and *chūdai* 中台 refer to two of the three stars that make up the "Purple Forbidden Enclosure" constellation, a group of stars close to north celestial pole that are associated with the emperor and high-ranked political offices. *Hōji Shōtoku Kōken kōtei* 宝字称徳孝謙皇帝 and *Tenpyō ōshin ninshō kōtaigō* 天平応真仁正皇太后 were formal titles for the emperor and empress dowager, respectively.

Emperor Shōtoku

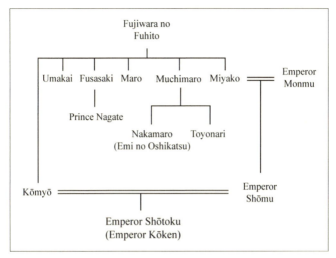

Lineage of Emperor Shōtoku

By Emperor Shōmu's orders, I, as a woman, inherited the throne so that the imperial line could continue. Though I passed the throne to the present emperor, he has not respectfully upheld it; he has said things that should not be said and done things that should not be done. Generally speaking, I do not recall his actions inviting criticism. Perhaps these accusations were made because I was living in a separate villa. With great shame, I feel that such allegations were made because of my own lack of virtue. On the other hand, I find that this is also an event of spiritual providence that shall affect my aspirations for Buddhahood. I therefore have taken the tonsure and become a Buddhist disciple. However, from now on, the rituals of the *kami* and small matters will be handled by the emperor, and I will preside over important affairs of the state and matters of justice.

With this, the Retired Emperor Kōken entered Hokkeji Temple, took the tonsure, and thus became the nun known as Hōkini.

Hearing this imperial decree, Nakamaro had his own plans. The previous alliance of Kōken and Nakamaro was now shifting to Nakamaro and Junnin. Dōkyō's appearance on the political scene was discomfiting for Nakamaro, and he secured his influence by gradually gathering followers and military force around him. In Tenpyō hōji 8 (764), Nakamaro attained an office with jurisdiction over military forces and issued a mobilization order to roughly 600 soldiers. The Senior Secretary of the Council of State, Takaoka no Hiramaro, was shocked to discover this and sent a secret message to Emperor Kōken. Nakamaro's residence was immediately surrounded. Nakamaro took his household staff with him and fled to Hora on the banks of Lake Biwa, but the emperor's people deployed an anti-Nakamaro force, and, in the end, Nakamaro's group lost their refuge. They met a miserable end on the eighth day of the ninth month. Retired Emperor Kōken was furious at Nakamaro, and even after the

Emperor Shōtoku   *213*

event, she issued imperial edicts again and again concerning how the situation was to be handled. Furthermore, on the morning of the ninth day of the tenth month, the Retired Emperor had Emperor Junnin's residence surrounded with soldiers. Not only because of Junnin's ineptitude as an emperor, but also because of his possible complicity with Nakamaro in his rebellion, Junnin was demoted from the position of emperor to crown prince and was exiled to the island of Awaji. Since then, Emperor Junnin's name has been left to history as the "Deposed Emperor" who was forced into abdication.

The Emergence of Emperor Shōtoku

According to the *Shoku Nihongi,* on the fourteenth day of the tenth month of 764, Emperor Takano (Emperor Kōken) gave the following reason for not establishing a crown prince: declaring a crown prince was necessary for the land, but for now, she had not decided on one because none of those presently thought to be good candidates were suitable. She thought that an appropriate person for the position of crown prince was one designated as such by heaven, so she would decide on someone shortly thereafter. No doubt the Nakamaro Incident weighed heavily on her mind.

Emperor Kōken once again ascended to the throne and became Emperor Shōtoku. Since Emperor Junnin had been

214

forced to abdicate, even though Kōken ascended to the throne, the usual ceremonies for imperial enthronement were not performed. As the new year began, on the seventh day of the first month, the era name was changed to Tenpyō jingo. When Emperor Junnin was enthroned, the era name was not changed from the previous Tenpyō hōji, an act that was without historical precedent in Japan. The Tenpyō hōji period was so-named for an auspicious omen in Kōken's time in which the words "*tenka taihei* ('great peace in the land,' taking the *ten* 天 character and *hei* 平 character, also read as *hyō/pyō*)" miraculously appeared on the ceiling of the the royal bedchamber, and several months later yet another auspicious omen occurred when numerous characters appeared woven onto silkworm cocoons.[80] The First Offering Harvest rites for Emperor Kōken as Emperor Shōtoku occurred on the twenty-third day of the eleventh month of that year.

As a part of the First Offering ceremony intended to announce the enthronement of the emperor to the land, there was also the custom of the Banquet of Abounding Light (*toyo*

---

[80] For a description of the characters that appeared and the interpretation of their message, see Ross Bender, "Changing the Calendar: Royal Political Theology and the Suppression of the Tachibana Naramaro Conspiracy of 757," *Japanese Journal of Religious Studies* 37, no. 2 (2010): 234-235.

no akari no sechi e).[81] After the rituals, at the so-called *naorai* (a ritual in which people share in the offering of sake and food made to the gods), the emperor ate some of the new grains and gave some of it to various retainers. There was then a *gosechi* dance, before grants and investitures were allotted. However, this occasion was unlike any before it. As the emperor herself had stated, she had already taken the tonsure and undertaken the precepts of the bodhisattva. Typically, people did not perceive buddhas as separate from *kami*; in sutras, *kami* are described as protectors of buddhas. Therefore, the emperor felt that even if a tonsured person mingled with laypeople and served the *kami*, this was not a hindrance or slight to efforts towards buddhahood. A consciousness of the syncretism of *kami* and buddha worship already permeated society, but at this banquet, monks and laity mixed to a degree that had not occurred before.

The Appearance of Dōkyō

Emperor Shōtoku's reign cannot be discussed without mentioning Dōkyō. The causes behind both the rebellion of Fujiwara no Nakamaro and the forced abdication of Emperor Junnin were also rooted in Dōkyō's presence. Dōkyō was

---

[81] See footnotes 33 and 74.

originally of the Yuge family of Kawachi province's Wakae district (present-day Yao City). The Yuge family had long been employed as bow-makers. At some point, Dōkyō took the tonsure and became a young disciple under the priest Gien. Gien was a high priest of the Hossō sect of Nara Buddhism and produced a large number of well-known disciples such as the priests Genpō, Gyōki, and Ryōben. Around Tenpyō 19 (747), Dōkyō was learning under Ryōben. He was already familiar with Sanskrit, and he was not only studying Buddhism but also Confucian learning. He also learned Zen as a Buddhist, as well as occult arts that were becoming popular at the time. It was thanks to these abilities and his extensive Buddhist training that Dōkyō could come and go at the imperial court as a nurse-monk. His first meeting with Emperor Shōtoku was also because of his skills as a nurse. Emperor Shōtoku, a single emperor who had lost her mother (the Empress Dowager Kōmyō) and had no siblings or children of her own, likely felt a deep sense of isolation when she became ill during her travels. Dōkyō was conveniently positioned to ease her loneliness.

On the fourth day of the ninth month of Tenpyō hōji 7 (763), Shōtoku issued an imperial order stating, "I appoint the priest Dōkyō to Junior Assistant Abbot (shōsōzu)." This appointment was to Yamashinaji (Kōfukuji) Temple. In the *Shoku Nihongi*, there is an article from 8.9.18 that provides an explanation for Nakamaro's rebellion, stating: "At that time,

Dōkyō served in the imperial court and received the emperor's particular favor. Nakamaro's heart was uneasy because of this." This was when Dōkyō was employed at the Hora residence as a nurse-monk for the emperor's illness. It suggests that he used his position then as an opportunity to become closer to the emperor, and this was a reason Nakamaro's rebellion occurred. On the twentieth day of the ninth month, Shōtoku issued an imperial edict. According to the edict, Nakamaro reported to the emperor that Dōkyō demonstrated considerable ambition and suggested that his influence be curbed, but, even so, her edict stated:

> Looking at this priest's conduct, it is very pure and meant to spread Buddhism; I cannot so easily dismiss such a priest who guides and protects me. Since I am conducting government as a tonsured emperor, I think it is permissible for a tonsured person to become cabinet minister. Priests want nothing for themselves, and I want the priest Dōkyō to receive the position of Buddhist Minister of State, so the various offices should recognize this decision.

Though abbreviated here, this imperial edict suggests various pretexts for Shōtoku's decision, and one can infer that the emperor favored Dōkyō. Two figures who allied themselves with Dōkyō and managed political administration were the

Minister of the Left, Fujiwara no Nagate (son of Fusasaki), and the Minister of the Right, Kibi no Makibi. Like Nakamaro, neither of them was from conspiratorial families, but were meek people, easily influenced by others. As a result, the reign of Emperor Shōtoku continued mainly under Dōkyō's leadership.

As an emperor who was also a devout believer in Buddhism, Emperor Shōtoku focused on supporting temples during her reign. One such project was the construction of Saidaiji Temple to the west in Nara, a task meant to complement the earlier building of Tōdaiji Temple to the east. As a large-scale construction project, it cost a considerable amount of human labor and impacted the state's financial affairs as well. On the eastern side of Nara, Sairyūji Temple (a nunnery) was also established, an act unsurprising for an emperor so dedicated to Buddhism.

Other than the construction of temples, Shōtoku also sponsored readings of sutras, the creation of Buddhist figures and pagodas, and civil engineering. On Tenpyō jingo 1 (765).10.13, Emperor Shōtoku left for Kii province, but on the way, she stopped at the Yamato Oharida residence, and on the eighteenth day arrived at Tamatsushima (a bay often featured in *waka* poetry). She stayed there around seven days. On her way back, she went to Kawachi province, and on the twenty-ninth day, she stopped at the imperial temporary lodging of the Yuge family. This was Dōkyō's

Emperor Shōtoku   *219*

hometown. There, Shōtoku gave Yugeji Temple 200
sustenance household grants.[82] Furthermore, she issued an
imperial edict that said Dōkyō was to be appointed to Great
Council of State. This was one month before the emperor
did the First Offering Harvest rites. In other words, she set
up her new administration with Dōkyō in a head position; for
Dōkyō, this was a kind of enthronement. Already the
emperor had come to believe that without Dōkyō she could
not run the government. The following year, the Buddha's
ashes were said to be miraculously discovered in the
Bishamonten statue at Sumidera Temple (also known as
Kairyūōji temple). The ashes were dedicated to Hokkeji
Temple. Since Dōkyō, a person who devoutly believed in
Buddhism and who worked for the prosperity of the Buddhist
law, was active at the time of this mysterious phenomenon,
the emperor praised him for his efforts after this event and
proclaimed he should receive the position of Dharma King
(*hōō*).[83] With easily manipulated figures occupying the

---

[82] See footnote 44.

[83] The title of Dharma King (*hōō* 法王) was a political position
created specifically for Dōkyō. A year prior, in 765, he had
already been named to another newly-created court position,
Buddhist Minister of State (*daijō daijin zenji* 太政大臣禅師),
which made the division between court authority and Buddhism
ambiguous.

positions of the Left and Right Ministers, Dōkyō thus solidified his grasp on the government and Shōtoku's reign continued its tranquil days. As in any period, exemptions from rice field taxes because of natural disasters were granted, and amnesties, investitures, rewards, and policies towards remote areas were also issued as usual.

In the eighth month of Tenpyō jingo 3 (767), the auspicious omen of five-color (or, depending on the place, seven-color) rainbow clouds appeared in the sky, so when the era name was changed, it became Jingo keiun, using the characters for *keiun* 景雲 meaning "scenery" and "clouds." The Dharma King Dōkyō continued to expand his authority. In the seventh month of Jingo keiun 3 (769), for the first time, he used his own Dharma King office seal on official documents, indicating his influence. Even before his unusual rise to power, the court surrounding Dōkyō experienced a number of unsettling incidents. For example, Prince Wake, the nephew of Emperor Junnin, was arrested for his involvement in the Nakamaro rebellion, and Princess Fuwa, Junnin's half-sister by another mother was caught trying to put a curse on the emperor. Dōkyō's involvement in the Usa Hachiman Incident, however, was more unsettling than these affairs.

The imperial family maintained devoted belief in the deity Usa Hachiman, and when Emperor Shōmu built the Daibutsu in the Heijō capital, it may have been at the behest of an oracle from Hachiman.[84] This time, an oracle from Hachiman stated that "If you make Dōkyō emperor, the land will have great peace." However, this was a false oracle prepared by the Usa Shintō priest Suge no Asomaro, and Emperor Shōtoku naturally had hesitations about somehow placing Dōkyō in the position of emperor. Shōtoku had a dream in which Hachiman commanded she send the nun Hōkin to determine the veracity of the oracle, and so she dispatched Hōkin's brother and her trusted official, Wake no Kiyomaro, to Usa. The oracle that Kiyomaro received and returned with stated: "Since the founding of our state, the distinction between ruler and subject has been fixed. Never has a subject been made a ruler. Unquestionably, only an emperor's heir shall be placed upon the imperial throne, and

---

[84] In the Nara period, it was believed that oracles were received from the Shintō deity Hachiman. According to Ross Bender, these oracles were of particular importance to the imperial family during this time as a way to obtain a syncretic balance of legitimacy between native customs of religion and rule and the increasingly vital connection between Buddhism and the state. For more on oracle customs, see Ross Bender, "Auspicious Omens in the Reign of the Last Empress of Nara Japan, 749-770," *Japanese Journal of Religious Studies* 40, no. 1 (2013): 45-76. For more on the theory that Shōmu built the *daibutsu* on behalf of Hachiman, see Bernard Scheid, "Shōmu Tennō and the Deity from Kyushu: Hachiman's Initial Rise to Prominence," *Japan Review* 27 (2014): 31-51.

wicked persons shall be immediately removed." Angered at this, Dōkyō punished Kiyomaro, and Kiyomaro's name was replaced in order to denigrate him. He became known as Wakebe no Kegaremaro (Kiyomaro meaning "pure man" and Kegaremaro meaning "defiled man"). He was also divested his position and banished to Oosumi province. His older sister, the nun Hōkin, too, was punished; her former name, Hiromushi (literally "wide insect") was changed to Samushi (literally "narrow insect"). She was forced into laity again and was exiled to Bingo. After the incident, Shōtoku issued a rather long edict, reiterating how trying her position had been until then.[85]

In the tenth month, the Emperor Shōtoku went to the Yuge residence, which she had used for some time as a villa, and made it the western capital. In the following year, once again she stopped there and stayed from the second month to the beginning of the fourth month; she had undoubtedly become quite fond of it. Of course, Dōkyō was also there with

---

[85] Although likely because of surrounding political pressure, it is unclear why exactly Shōtoku did not turn against Dōkyō, allowed him to punish Kiyomaro and Hōkin, or, conversely, proceed with the original oracle to name Dōkyō emperor. Ross Bender has written an excellent summary and analysis of this complex situation in "The Hachiman Cult and the Dokyo Incident," *Monumenta Nipponica* 34, no. 2 (Summer 1979): 142-144.

her to conduct government affairs. In the sixth month, the emperor, whose physical condition had declined, returned to Heijō palace, and on the fourth day of the eighth month, she died at Nishi no miya. She was fifty-three years old.

The emperor was single her entire life and never decided upon a crown prince. Therefore, the Minister of the Left, Fujiwara Nagate, Minister of the Right, Kibi no Makibi, and other the courtiers gathered and hurriedly made Prince Shirakabe (Emperor Tenji's grandson and the eldest among the princes) the crown prince. The new crown prince was restricted to the Heijō palace, and Dōkyō to a hermitage close to the late emperor's tomb. In the eighth month, the crown prince charged Dōkyō with conspiring to seize the throne, but given Dōkyō's history of meritorious deeds, there was no conviction. Instead, he was exiled to be a steward to Yakushiji Temple in Shimozuke province.

Emperor Shōtoku's life was tumultuous. When she was the crown prince under the patronage of her father, Emperor Shōmu, it was comparatively peaceful, and during her time as Emperor Kōken, she had the guardianship of her mother, Empress Dowager Kōmyō. After Empress Dowager Kōmyō died, however, she was betrayed by the well-trusted Nakamaro; one can tell from the many opportunities she took to bring up his name and lay blame on him in her imperial edicts that this betrayal deeply wounded her. The one who comforted her was Dōkyō. We cannot know if Dōkyō was aiming for the imperial throne from the beginning, but both the emperor's vulnerable circumstances and Dōkyō's lust for power led to a great deal of instability in the government.

Although Emperor Shōtoku's history with Dōkyō is the first association that comes to mind when speaking of her life and reign, the emperor also had a deep knowledge of Confucianism, left behind Chinese poetry in the *Keikokushū*, and excelled at writing. In Tōshōdaiji Temple there are surviving placards by temple founders (*mongaku*) and documents written in the emperor's own hand. The remaining examples of her superb calligraphy are full of majesty.

Emperor Kōken/Shōtoku's personality and political attitudes seem to have changed over the fifteen years of her two reigns. As Emperor Kōken, she was under the protection of her mother, Empress Dowager Kōmyō, and was deeply devoted to her. Under the influence of her father, Emperor Shōmu, she seemed to be of a devoutly Buddhist and tranquil character. However, she became quite assertive after the Nakamaro Incident in 764, having felt betrayed and isolated as a result of the conflict. As the tonsured Shōtoku, the emperor came to rely heavily on Dōkyō, a contrast to her previous self-possessed nature. Even so, Shōtoku had not waited quietly for her own son, grandson, or nephew to take the imperial throne, nor did she fulfill the role of intermediary to dislodge opposing influences; rather, from the outset, she was the first female crown prince. She became emperor and further took hold of political power as retired emperor. Shōtoku then reascended the throne as emperor, and, in the end, never decided upon a successor.

Although the first six female emperors reigned before or during the Nara period, the next female emperor did not appear until 859 years later, at the beginning of the Tokugawa period.

Emperor Meishō

(r. 1629-1643)

Translated by Paula R. Curtis

Grandchild of the second shogun, Hidetada.
The female emperor who was
enthroned at age seven and
became retired emperor at twenty-one.

There were no female emperors from the end of Emperor Shōtoku's reign in 770 until Emperor Meishō's emergence in the Tokugawa period (1603-1868). Emperor Meishō was the seventh female emperor and 109th overall. Second daughter of the 108th emperor, Emperor Go-Mizuno'o (r. 1611-1629), her mother Kazuko (also read as Masako, and later named Tōfukumon-in) was a daughter of the second shogun, Hidetada (1579-1632). Meishō's personal name was Okiko and while she was young, she was referred to by the title Onna ichi no miya. She was born in Genna 9 (1623), and in Kan'ei 6 (1629) she received an imperial proclamation conferring her the title of "imperial princess (*naishinnō*)." Meishō was enthroned the following year, at the age of only seven. Naturally, there were extenuating circumstances behind this enthronement. Before explaining these events, first let us touch on her mother's entry into court as an imperial consort.[86]

Kazuko (Tōfukumon-in) 's presentation as an imperial consort

While Tokugawa Ieyasu (1543-1616) worked to reinforce the foundations of the newly established Tokugawa bakufu, he also launched more personal ambitions, plotting a way to satisfy his long-held desire for a daughter of the Tokugawa family to enter the imperial household. Ieyasu wished to emulate the Heian period example of Taira no Kiyomori (1118-1181), who made his daughter, Tokuko, empress to Emperor Takakura, resulying in the birth of a son, who became the next emperor, Antoku (r. 1180-1185). Minamoto no Yoritomo (1147-1199) also requested that his first daughter be made Emperor Go-Toba's empress, but she

---

[86] Translated here as "imperial consort," *judai* 入内 refers to the process by which an empress or court lady undertakes formal rites or customary procedures in order to enter the imperial palace for the first time. These formalities were necessary to formally induct the woman into the court and place her as a consort/attendant to the emperor, often with an understanding that she may become empress.

lacked rank, so the match never came to fruition. In contrast, Kiyomori had Tokuko properly presented at court as an imperial consort for the Retired Emperor Go-Shirakawa's nephew (adopted son), so there were no issues regarding her position. Moreover, there was also a need for the court to form marriages with the Taira family at that time. This example stuck in Ieyasu's mind, and he desired to someday gain the position of maternal grandfather to the emperor just as the former Fujiwara regency family had done through marriage into the imperial family. On the surface, his goals appeared to be an official alliance that would ensure the smooth functioning of the administration, but, undoubtedly, Ieyasu lusted for power greater than a simple alliance.

Ieyasu's goal to marry a daughter into the imperial family was not achieved during his lifetime but became possible during the rule of the second shogun, Hidetada, who had five daughters. Ieyasu wished for the fifth daughter, Kazuko, to be made an imperial consort to Emperor Go-Mizuno'o. Kazuko was born in Keichō 12 (1607), and her mother was Yodogimi's younger sister Oeyo. From a young age, she was a quick-witted and beautiful girl. At two years old, it was already rumored that she would soon be presented to the court as an imperial consort. Imperial orders to that effect were issued in Keichō 19 (1614), during the fourth month of Kazuko's eighth year. Two messengers from Kyoto came to Ieyasu in Sunpu and conveyed the court's will that

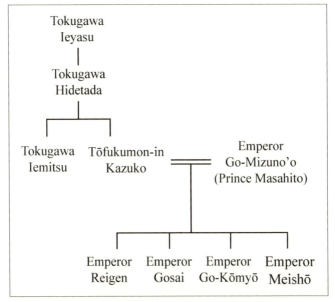

Lineage of Emperor Meishō

Kazuko be presented and Ieyasu be conferred the titles of Chancellor and *Junsangō*,[87] but Ieyasu only accepted the offer of Kazoku's position and refused the offices for himself. With this, Kazuko was accepted into the court as the emperor's consort.

Despite this successful arrangement, the political

---

[87] *Junsangō* 准三后 was a title granted to high officials that provided the holder with economic revenue equivalent to that of three empresses.

situation of the time was unstable. First, there was the winter campaign of the Siege of Osaka in the tenth month of 1614, and the summer campaign in the following year, when the Toyotomi family was destroyed. The era name was changed that year to Genna. Soon after, in the fourth month of 1616, Ieyasu died, and the year after that, the Emperor Go-Yōzei died. These events delayed Kazuko's entrance as imperial consort. Finally, in 1619, her presentation was decided upon and preparations begun. However, there were other troublesome circumstances surrounding her future role.

Hidetada, who had already entered the capital to introduce his to the court, heard news that a princess, Ume no miya, had been born to one of the female attendants of the emperor, who was known as the "Oyotsu Mistress." The mistress Oyotsu had already given birth to the prince Kamo no miya in the previous year, and both had gone to her hometown and were living in secret to avoid inciting further tension over the bakufu's plans for Kazuko.

Having children with a woman other than one's official wife was not an unusual thing in this time period, and the emperor was also not limited to a single partner. However, the timing of the affair made Hidetada displeased, since he was about to present his beloved daughter to the emperor. Kazuko's entrance into the court was immediately postponed, and after Hidetada, in frustration, punished the courtiers who ordered the delay, the matter appeared to be resolved. The

Tokugawa bakufu also issued the seventeen-article "Regulations for the Imperial Court and Nobility (*kinchū narabi ni kuge shohatto*)" around this time.[88] Emperor Go-Mizuno'o was displeased with the bakufu's various actions, and for a time spoke of abdicating. However, this also settled down and in the sixth month of the eighteenth day of Genna 6 (1620), Kazuko was at last presented.

This was the first time a woman of the shogunal family entered the court as an imperial consort, so the event was a very luxurious and splendid affair. With expenses amounting to 700,000 *koku* (about 100,000,000,000 yen),[89] the ceremony was more than enough to showcase the influence of the bakufu to the imperial court.

---

[88] The *Kinchū narabi ni kuge shohatto* 禁中並公家諸法度 was a set of seventeen articles issued in 1615 by Tokugawa Ieyasu to the imperial court. Traditionally, scholars interpreted it as a restrictive document that placed strict regulations on the court and enhanced bakufu control over imperial affairs. However, as research by historian Lee Butler shows, this document was not significantly different from other documents issued by the bakufu to the court in the previous decade, and consisted largely of reaffirmations of required court customs, culture, and responsibilities that had centuries-old precedent. See Lee Butler, *Emperor and Aristocracy in Japan: 1467-1680* (Cambridge: Harvard University Press, 2002), 198-224.

[89] At an exchange rate of approximately 124 USD to yen, 800 million USD.

Kazuko, now a fourteen-year old consort, was far from her hometown of Edo. Along with a small number of retainers brought with her to Kyoto, she had to adjust to a new lifestyle in an environment not unlike a foreign country, where everyday life and even the language were entirely different from what she knew. Separated from her husband, the emperor, Kazuko began her daily life in the Empress's Palace (*nyōgo gosho*), and three years later, in Genna 9 (1623), their daughter Onna ichi no miya (who would later become Emperor Meishō), was born. Kazuko also gave birth to two princes and four more princesses. In Kan'ei 1 (1624), the year after Kazuko gave birth to Ichi no miya, she officially received the title of *chūgū*, recognizing her as a legitimate wife and empress consort of the emperor. Friction often occurred between the court and the bakufu from the conception of Hidetada's plan to present Kazuko to the court until the enthronement of Emperor Meishō, friction that was only amplified by other problematic affairs within the court.

Until Emperor Go-Mizuno'o's Abdication

A great number of significant events occurred during the reign of Emperor Go-Mizuno'o, Emperor Meishō's father. He passed his early years as Imperial Prince Masahito, third son of Emperor Go-Yōzei (1586-1611). In Keichō 16 (1611), Go-Mizuno'o was enthroned after Emperor Go-Yōzei's abdication. Go-Mizuno'o's enthronement also reflected the will of Tokugawa Ieyasu, given that he wished for Kazuko to be presented to Go-Mizuno'o as an imperial consort. Since it was undiginified for an emperor to have the presentation of his consort postponed due to his own "misconduct" in the Oyotsu affair, Emperor Go-Mizuno'o expressed his desire to abdicate. However, if he did so, the bakufu's long-standing objective to present Kazuko to the court would become meaningless. So Hidetada instead punished the emperor's attendants, sending three courtiers into exile. Hearing this, the emperor wished to take responsibility himself and once again stated his will to abdicate, but Hidetada prevented him from doing so.[90] When Kazuko finally became a lady of the court, the matter was tentatively settled, but the bakufu's ability to impose its will on the court continued and the court's resentment towards the bakufu (and warrior groups as a whole) lingered.

Emperor Go-Mizuno'o's next urge to abdicate occurred because of the intrusion of the bakufu in court affairs during the so-called "Purple Robe Incident (*shie jiken*)." A *shie* is a purple-colored article of clothing, a kind of monk or priest's stole (*kesa*). Purple stoles in particular were only allowed to

---

[90] For more on these events, see Elizabeth Lillehoj and John T. Carpenter, and John T. Carter, *Art and Palace Politics in Early Modern Japan, 1580s-1680s* (Boston: Brill, 2014), 126-127.

be worn by high-ranking priests who had been granted an imperial sanction from the court. Although the Tokugawa bakufu was already imposing numerous policies on various Buddhist sects, controversy erupted in response to the bakufu's claim to jurisdiction over the granting of purple robes.

In Keichō 18 (1613), the bakufu created a law requiring that to become chief priests of the eight high-status temples (such as Daitokuji, Myōshinji, Chion'in, etc.), who were allowed by imperial sanction to wear purple robes, consent from the bakufu was necessary before imperial approval could be received. Additionally, in Genna 1 (1615), the bakufu issued the "Regulations for the Imperial Court and Nobility" and made the rules regulating temples even stricter. These were regulations aimed at curbing arbitrary imperial approvals of purple robes and priestly titles, but it is true that temples were also in a state of disarray at the time. The Rinzai sect's Daitokuji and Myōshinji temples were singled out in particular, and in the seventh month of Kan'ei 4 (1627), the bakufu revoked imperial permissions issued from the Genna period onward. In response to this punishment, the priest Takuan of Daitokuji Temple rebelled, and troubles surrounding the issue continued. Emperor Go-Mizuno'o expressed his anger towards the situation. Hosokawa Tadaoki, a loyal follower of the Tokugawa, said of this: "There is no greater shame for the emperor than this matter."

Emperor Meishō   235

This incident became an opportunity for the emperor to once again decide to abdicate, and this time the bakufu had no desire to stop him since the empress had given birth to an imperial prince, Sukehito. The emperor therefore began construction of the *Sentō gosho*, the post-abdication residence. However, in the sixth month of the following year, the imperial prince Sukehito suddenly died; he was only three years old. The empress, who was pregnant at the time, gave birth to the second imperial prince in the ninth month, but he, too, died at only nine days old. Over and over the imperial family suffered great misfortune, and once again the abdication of Emperor Go-Mizuno'o was postponed. Amidst this turmoil, in the fifth month of Kan'ei 6 (1629), the emperor finally abdicated, but this time for reasons of illness.

Go-Mizuno'o was suffering from a tumor as well as full-body paralysis. Though the court physician Nakarai Tsūsen-in gave him medicine, it was unhelpful. Moxibustion was an effective remedy, but the process would have caused physical wounds to the emperor's body, which was not allowed.[91] Chūkamon-in (Go-Mizuno'o's mother) and the court discussed whether Go-Mizuno'o should abdicate. Ultimately, they sent

---

[91] Moxibustion is a medicinal treatment originating in traditional Chinese medicine. In direct moxibustion, mugwort is ground up into cone shapes and burned on the skin at acupuncture points to affect circulation and the energies of the body.

word to the bakufu stating that there were standing precedents of female emperors being enthroned, and so Okiko should succeed Go-Mizuno'o. The bakufu did not reply right away, and the reply that finally did come said that they should avoid a female emperor and await the birth of a prince. The empress was pregnant.

Emperor Go-Mizuno'o was dissatisfied, if not angry, with the bakufu's repeated hardline stance, and it is thought that his true intention was to quickly abdicate. With such terrible events piling up and various troubles with the bakufu transpiring, again and again incidents occurred that made the emperor resentful. Another such incident was Kasuga no Tsubone's palace visit.

Kasuga no Tsubone was a woman named Fuku who had been involved in Tokugawa Iemitsu (r. 1623-1651)'s education since infancy as his wet nurse. She was thus deeply trusted by the shogun Iemitsu, and in Edo, she held such great influence that nearly everyone knew her name. However, having no special rank or title, she was a person of humble birth who could not be expected to enter the court or courtier society. However, taking on the role of Senior Counselor Sanjōnishi Sane'eda's adopted sister, Fuku was able to visit the imperial court for an audience with the emperor and received a sake cup as a gift. She also received the name "Kasuga no Tsubone" from the empress. To the courtiers, this audience with someone so common was something that insulted the

Emperor Meishō   *237*

dignity of the emperor. Having to do whatever the bakufu said pushed the emperor's pride and anger to its utmost limits. A poem on the emperor's mental state shows that he wished to abdicate as soon as possible, if he had to endure this kind of insult:

> my sleeves, soaked
> with tears from my
> grieving for the world,
> and the moon, all but clouded over,
> are both filled with sorrow[92]

yo o nageku / namida gachi naru / tamoto ni wa /
kumoru bakari no / tsuki mo kanashiki

On the morning of the eighth day of the eleventh month, the emperor issued a sudden summons to the courtiers. In this summons, the emperor proclaimed that his throne would be passed to imperial princess Onna ichi no miya Okiko. This announcement was completely unexpected. Neither the imperial princess herself nor the empress, Kazuko, had been notified beforehand. Of course, nothing was said to the shogun, Hidetada, either. Hidetada was angry to be left out of

---

[92] The original author does not include a citation for the poetic collection in which this poem appears.

this process and did not immediately give his consent, but before long, he sent a reply stating that he would respect the emperor's will. While Hidetada was uncomfortable with the emperor ignoring the bakufu when making this important decision, on the other hand, he probably held a deep sense of satisfaction that his own grandchild would become emperor. With this abrupt abdication, 859 years after the female rulers of the Nara period, a new female emperor, Emperor Meishō, was enthroned.

The Time of Emperor Meishō

The rites for the sudden abdication of Emperor Go-Mizuno'o and the enthronement of Imperial Princess Okiko were held ten months later, on the twelfth day of the ninth month of Kan'ei 7 (1630) in the Ceremonial Hall (*shishinden*). It was the first time there was a seven-year-old female emperor. Male child emperors were the rule throughout the Fujiwara regency in the Heian period, the *insei* period,[93] and centuries that followed in which warriors frequently dominated various aspects of political administration. So there was little expectation that that the seven-year-old girl would truly act as the emperor and it was assumed that the

---

[93] See footnote 4.

responsibility of rule would be assumed by the regents and advisors.

An emperor had a number of duties. First, divine work; court rituals and other annual ceremonial events could be performed only by the emperor. Additionally, there was also the granting of investiture, medals of merit, and the awarding of offices, etc. Even though the word "shogun" is often used to refer to a person, it actually refers to the office of *Seiitai daishōgun* (The Great General Who Subdues Eastern Barbarians), which was chosen by the emperor. In addition to this kind of official work, the emperor had numerous responsibilities in regards to education. The emperor was expected to be accomplished in the Chinese classics, knowledge of the achievements of past emperors, and also classical literature, waka, calligraphy, and music. There were also audiences with the emperor and imperial visits, requirements not easily handled by one as young as Meishō. Therefore, regents and advisors managed public matters of the court. The retired emperor immediately moved to the empress' residence (*chūgū gosho*) and Kazuko was awarded the empress dowager title Tōfukumon-in. The retired emperor was thirty-four years old, and he died at the age of eighty-five.

Politics, economics, and diplomacy were all under the bakufu's control, and it happened that a great many significant historical events took place during Meishō's reign, beginning with the Shimabara Rebellion in response to prohibitions on Christianity, trade relations with Holland and Portugal, and the solidification of the alternate attendance system.[94] It was a critical period for Japan and the Tokugawa bakufu. Emperor Meishō was emperor from Kan'ei 6 to 20 (1629-1643), for thirteen years and eleven months.

On the third day of the tenth month of Kan'ei 20 (1643), Emperor Meishō passed the throne to her younger half-brother (by Suga-no-miya Tsuguhito), who thus became Emperor Go-Kōmyō. Emperor Meishō, who became retired emperor, was called the "new retired emperor," and began a tranquil life.

Emperor Meishō's Life after Retirement

From age twenty-one, Emperor Meishō remained single and led her life as a retired emperor while the throne passed to emperors Go-Kōmyō (r. 1643-1654), Gosai (r. 1655-1663), Reigen (r. 1663-1687), and Higashiyama (r. 1687-1709).

---

[94] The alternate attendance (*sankin kōtai* 参勤交代) system was a control mechanism utilized by the Tokugawa bakufu. Daimyo were required to alternate years in attendance in the capital of Edo, using personal funds to travel from their (sometimes distant) domains and leaving their families hostage in the capital when not in residence.

Other than Higashiyama, they were all younger brothers from different mothers. During Meishō's time, the bakufu was instituting rather detailed regulations for retired emperors, and amidst that restrictive daily life, Meishō's only comfort was going out to the Shūgakuin villa with her tonsured father and her mother Tōfukumon-in. There, she diligently occupied herself with artistic crafts, and many of those works, such as her *oshie* (raised cloth pictures), survive today in Kyoto's notable temples. Meishō also had deep faith in Buddhism, and she was devoted to the priest Kōgyoku Jōkei, who restored the Yamashina Jūzenji Temple, that had been ruined by the fires of war. In Meireki 1 (1655), because of a dream, Meishō made Jūzenji Temple a place of prayer and donated a great deal of money and goods to it.

In Genroku 9 (1696), Meishō died at the age of seventy-four. Her imperial tomb is the Tsuki no wa tomb of Senyūji Temple. Emperor Meishō's imperial name was, by the emperor's will, taken from the two names of the Nara-period female emperors Genmei and Genshō. In the year before her death, Meishō ordered that her private Buddhist figure, used for personal worship, be left to Jūzenji. Meishō's personal letters to Kōgyoku Jōkei exhibit beautiful handwriting, the old poems she wrote on colored paper were done in bold calligraphy, and the characters of her handcopied Zuigudarani and Lotus sutras are clearly and precisely written. Furthermore, the plaque inscriptions of Jūzenji Temple, done when she was sixty-seven years old, are by and large filled with a sublime spirit, and do not feel as if they were written by an aged woman who spent her lifetime deep in the palace. A graceful kindness and tenacious spirit were hidden in this noblewoman who was treated as an instrument of the government.

The retired emperor also left her treasured *amagatsu* dolls and *hōko* dolls[95] to Jūzenji Temple. In addition, in *Ranpūjō*, there is something called the *Tennō shinkan koka onjikishi* (Colored Paper with the Emperor's Old Poem), and on that, there is the following poem:

> it's a long way
> to the hills where
> the mists of spring are rising,
> but the blowing breeze
> brings scents of spring

---

[95] *Amagatsu* 天児 (literally "heavenly child") are a kind of talismanic doll, made with a round head and a body of crossed bamboo sticks, typically adorned with white silk robes. *Hōko* 這子 (literally, "crawling child") are very similar, though they resemble a child crawling on their hands and feet and are often stuffed. Both are intended as protective charms for mothers and children.

kasumi tatsu / haru no yamabe wa / tookeredo /
fuki kuru kaze wa / haru no ka no suru

During Emperor Meishō's time, political administration
was in the hands of the Tokugawa bakufu, so there was
nothing related to governance for the emperor to do herself.
Even if there were an inquiry from the bakufu, Emperor Go-
Mizuno'o would most likely address it, leaving nothing for
Meishō to manage. Meishō's fourteen-year reign at the
palace, from the time she was a little girl to when she was a
young woman, was a splendid period, but her voice as an
emperor was never heard. Unlike the female emperors that
reigned until the Nara period, there was no need for Emperor
Meishō to proclaim imperial decrees before hundreds of
officials. And because she had a younger brother who would
quietly become the next emperor, she abdicated when she was
requested to do so. Emperor Meishō was an intermediary
emperor not of her own will.

Column 7

Picked Radish and String Beans

Takuan (also known as Sōhō), who was a central

figure in the Purple Robe Incident that occurred in the reign of Emperor Go-Mizuno'o, held a central role in the Rinzai temple Daitokuji. When the bakufu instigated the Purple Robe Incident, Takuan took initiative in support of the imperial court, sending his opinions in writing to the bakufu. The bakufu, taking no heed of them, exiled Takuan to Kamiyama, located in Dewa province. Later pardoned, he lectured on Buddhism in the imperial court, and even received bakufu support to establish the Tōkaiji temple in Shinagawa, Edo. It is thought that Takuan also pickled radishes, so today pickled radishes are called *takuanzuke* (literally, "Takuan pickles").

Meanwhile, Ingen (Yinyuan Longqi) was a Chinese monk of the Ming Dynasty Ōbakushū (a Zen Buddhist school). He came to Japan in Jōō 3 (1654) at the age of sixty-three and built Manpukuji Temple in Uji, Yamashiro province (Kyoto), becoming the founder of the Ōbaku School in Japan. It is said that Ingen brought *ingenmame* (string beans) with him when he came to Japan. Both *takuanzuke* and *ingenmame*, now familiar items on the Japanese table, are foods adopted during Emperor Meishō's lifetime.

Emperor Go-Sakuramachi
(r. 1762-1771)

Translated by Paula R. Curtis

A female emperor of conviction who
thoughtfully attended to the court.

Emperor Go-Sakuramachi was the eighth female emperor. Born on Genbun 5. 8. 3 (1740) as the second princess of Emperor Sakuramachi (r. 1735-1747), her mother was Sakuramachi's consort Ieko, who was the daughter of the *kanpaku*[96] Nijō Yoshitada. Go-Sakuramachi's personal name was Toshiko (originally Satoko), her pre-accession title was Isa no miya, and she was also later known as Ake no miya. In the third month of Kan'en 3 (1750), she was conferred the title of imperial princess by imperial proclamation.

---

[96] *Kanpaku* 関白 was a kind of regent position for an adult emperor.

Until Enthronement

Emperor Sakuramachi (the 115th emperor) and Ieko had a first daughter, Miki no miya, in Genbun 2 (1737), but she died when she was ten years old. This was one reason that Ake no miya became the Go-Sakuramachi emperor so soon. In the second month of Kanpo 1 (1741), half a year after Ake no miya's birth, Emperor Sakuramachi sired a prince, Yaho no miya (birth mother Tenji no Anekōji Sadako), but no prince had been born to Ieko, so in the tenth month of Enkyō 2 (1745), she adopted Yaho no miya (renamed Saji no miya), making him Ake no miya's younger brother. In the third month of Enkyō 3, he was named Mōke no kimi (imperial successor), and in the fifth month of Enkyō 4 (1747) became the crown prince. With the abdication of Emperor Sakuramachi, Saji no miya, six years old, ascended to the throne to become Emperor Momozono (r. 1747-1762). However, the retired emperor Sakuramachi died three years later in 1750 at the age of thirty-one, and his adoptive mother, the Empress Dowager, took guardianship of the child emperor Momozono as Seikimon-in. The rule of the young emperor lasted for sixteen years, until his death at the age of twenty-two. The next prince to inherit the throne was the first imperial prince Hidehito, born in Hōreki 8 (1758), but he was only five years old and still too young for the throne. Historically, there had been young emperors, but usually their grandfathers or great-

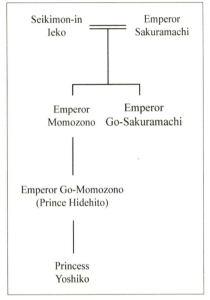

Lineage of Emperor Go-Sakuramachi

grandfathers would handle government affairs as their guardian. There were no elderly retired emperors or imperial family members there to provide support at this time. Furthermore, unlike the Heian regency period of government, the government during this period was entirely under the control of the bakufu and the emperor did not directly rule.

The courtiers in Kyoto and Seikimon-in discussed placing the imperial princess Ake no miya, the young imperial prince Hidehito's aunt, on the throne until he reached the age of ten. This suggestion was motivated in part by the Hōreki

Incident of 1758, which occurred during the reign of Emperor Momozono. In this affair, a number of young courtiers, Emperor Momozono among them, were influenced by Takenouchi Shikibu's anti-bakufu imperial loyalist ideology based on the Suika Shinto of Yamazaki Ansai (1618-1682).[97] The more established courtiers within the imperial court opposed these teachings, and, in the end, more than twenty of Takenouchi Shikibu's adherents were punished and Shikibu was exiled. Thus, the people of the court felt anxious about the kind of backing a young emperor would receive. Seikimon-in was of the opinion that imperial prince Hidehito should become emperor even if he was young, but she had to accede to the strong wishes of the court, and the bakufu also consented to Ake no miya's inheritance of throne. Therefore, on the twenty-seventh day of the seventh month of Hōreki 12 (1761), Ake no miya became Emperor Go-Sakuramachi.

---

[97] Yamazaki Ansai, a Neo-Confucian scholar, advocated Suika Shintō, a form of Confucianist Shintō that combined post-medieval Shintō ideas with the theoretical teachings of Chinese philosopher Zhu Xi. His emphasis on ethical and moral behavior underpinning proper worship of native *kami* greatly influenced pro-imperial support and reaffirmed notions of the emperor's divinity.

Enthronement and Life on the Throne

Emperor Go-Sakuramachi's enthronement ceremonies occurred in Hōreki 13 (1763). 11. 27. The First Offering Harvest rites were also held on the eighth day of the eleventh month of the following year, Meiwa 1 (1764). These rites (a ceremony of the year's first grain offering, also called *oonie no matsuri*) were a large, once-in-a-lifetime celebration that had been discontinued in the Muromachi period (1336-1573). They were revived during the Tokugawa period under the 113th emperor, Emperor Higashiyama, and thus did not occur during the reign of the Emperor Meishō. This event was reported to be the first instance in which Emperor Go-Sakuramachi wore ceremonial robes as the female emperor. Enthroned at age twenty-two, Go-Sakuramachi, was, from the beginning, an intermediary emperor until her nephew Hidehito matured and could be enthroned. Although Go-Sakuramachi became an intermediary, unlike the ancient female emperors, she was not enthroned out of her strong will to protect the throne through her own bloodline or until her son reached maturity. Rather, all of these decisions were determined by those around her.

Go-Sakuramachi left behind a diary, *Go-Sakuramachi tennō shinki*. The diary covers twenty-five years, from the first month of Hōreki 6 (1756, before her enthronement) to the first month of An'ei 9 (1780). An extremely valuable historical resource, the work stretches from Emperor Go-Sakuramachi's time as imperial princess to the period in which she was recognized as emperor. She writes in detail about her official business, including her thoughts on her young nephew's abdication and details on an emperor's everyday life. Go-Sakuramachi was a person who, even as a young emperor, was very self-aware of her role. Although she was conscious of her role an intermediary for her nephew, she meticulously carried out her duties as emperor during her reign.

On Meiwa 5 (1768).2.19, imperial prince Hidehito was invested as the crown prince, and on the ninth day of the eighth month he had his coming-of-age ceremony. On Meiwa 7 (1770). 11. 24, Emperor Go-Sakuramachi abdicated as intended, and imperial prince Hidehito was enthroned as the Emperor Go-Momozono (r. 1771-1779). After a reign of only eight years, Emperor Go-Sakuramachi retired as emperor at age thirty.

Emperor Go-Momozono was sickly from birth, and he died in An'ei 8 (1779), nine years after his enthronement. Imperial Princess Yoshiko had only just been born, and her younger brother, the imperial prince Sadayuki, had died, so Prince Sachi no miya, son of the Imperial Prince Kan'in no miya Sukehito (great-grandchild of Emperor Higashiyama), was enthroned and became Emperor Kōkaku. However, during these transitional times, the various imperial duties rested squarely on the shoulders of the retired Emperor Go-Sakuramachi, who was the heart of the imperial household.

Many political issues took place in Go-Sakuramachi's time. One such matter was the Meiwa Incident. During the rule of the tenth shogun, Ieharu, a Confucian scholar of the Yamazaki Ansai school of thought named Yamagata Daini opened a school in Edo and gave lectures on military strategy, Confucianism, and customs of military and court households while promoting anti-bakufu thought in, as he saw it, defense of the national polity. This was discovered by the bakufu and Daini was arrested and put to death. During the previous Hōreki Incident, Takenouchi Shikibu had been banished to the island of Hachijō, and conflicts such as these allowed imperialist ideologies to gain further popularity. In addition, riots similar to the *ikki* uprisings were occurring in various areas, and this was the period in which the influential politician Tanuma Okitsugu[98] was active.

The literary and artistic achievments of this period reflect the changing tastes of the court and bakufu. Literary works such as Karai Senryū's *Yanagitaru* and Ueda Akinari's

---

[98] Tanuma Okitsugu (1718-1788) was a highly influential advisor to the shogun Tokugawa Ieharu (r. 1760-1786). During his time in office, he wielded exceptional power over government policy in a variety of affairs, from appointments to government positions and economic development to foreign trade.

Ugetsu monogatari were published, and the *nishiki-e* (multi-colored woodblock printing) of Suzuki Harunobu had begun to be produced. Kamo no Mabuchi, the famed poet and *kokugaku* scholar, also died during the time of Emperor Go-Sakuramachi.[99]

In addition to her aforementioned diary, Emperor Go-Sakuramachi wrote *Kinchū nenjū no koto*. This work was written in *kana* script and, beginning with the Four Direction Prayer (*shihōhai*) ceremony of the new year, covered imperial court customs until the last day of the twelfth month. In addition, there was the *Rakugai gokō omichisuji kakitsuke*, a detailed account of Emperor Reigen (112th emperor)'s round-trip route on an imperial visit to Shūgakuin, an imperial villa.

Go-Sakuramachi also produced the *kana* work *Kokindenju no gyoki* in Meiwa 4. 3. 24 (1767), which was about the instruction in the secrets of *waka* poetry from Imperial Prince Arisugawa no miya Yorihito. Talented at imperial *waka* traditions, the emperor frequently held poetry parties at the court. These poems were collected as imperial poems from Meiwa 1 (1751), the year following her enthronement, until the emperor's death in Bunka 10 (1813). The 28-volume *Go-Sakuramachi tennō gyosei* features 1,588

---

[99] *Kokugaku* 国学, literally "study of [our] country," was a nativist intellectual movement focused on philology and philosophy that emerged in Tokugawa Japan.

Emperor Go-Sakuramachi   *253*

poems, from which we can know the emperor's most profound sentiments. This is the first poem included:

> every passing spring
> shows even more color
> in the world of our sovereign,
> the flourishing world pledged
> by the branches of pine

> iku haru mo / nao iro soeyo / suberagino /
> yoyo no sakae o / chigiru matsu ga e
>
> [GSTG Hōreki 14.1.24]

The poem's topic is the "Pine, Color, Spring, Longevity" Imperial Poetry Party (*gokaihajime*) from the fourteenth day of the first month. In other words, it is a poem composed on a set theme, in this case, typical topics for a poetry competition at the beginning of a new year. The poem suggests the newly enthroned emperor's sense of aspiration. The following poem is the last from the imperial poetry collection:

> these flowers have bloomed —
> their color and fragrance!
> to show that spring has come —
>> the other trees too must have

started to put forth their buds

haru kinu to / sakuya kono hana / iro mo ka mo /
koto ki to megumu / hajime naruran

[GSTG Bunka 10.1.18]

This is an imperial poem from the first month of Bunka 10
(1813), when Emperor Go-Sakuramachi was seventy-four
years old. She had entered old age and the spring of the new
year was particularly full of deep emotions for her. The poem
below was composed during her travels in Tenmei 7 (1789):

I hear their voices as friends
as flocks of plovers call to each other,
friends seeking friends,
as I travel to an unknown place
sleeping on a pillow of waves

mura chidori / tomo sasou koe o / tomo to kiku /
shiranu tabine no / nami no makura ni

[GSTG Tenmei 7.6.22]

It is not certain to where she traveled, but the poem evokes a
sense of pathos in the loneliness of a night sleeping alone in a
strange land. In addition, there are also the following poems,
in which one can sense her heartfelt emotions:

Emperor Go-Sakuramachi   *255*

those fallen blossoms
floating at the whim of the water
of the flowing river
seem to have become
the very spirit of the wind

yuku kawa no / mizu no ma ni ma ni / chiri ukabu /
hana koso kaze no / kokoro naru rashi

[GSTG Meiwa 4.2.2]

without my noticing
almost ten autumns have passed
and unaware
I have grown familiar with
the moon above the clouds

itsu tomonaku / totose ni chikaki / aki o hete /
omowazu naruru / kumo no ue no tsuki

[GSTG Meiwa 7.7.24]

Similarly, there is the following poem:

how might I express
the accumulated feelings
of waiting night after night
for the person

on whom I relied

tanome okishi / hito o matsu mi no / yo goro kaku /
tsumoru omoi o / ikade shirasemu

[GSTG Meiwa 7.3.24]

This poem's topic is "waiting for someone," and poignantly expresses the secret feelings of the emperor. Like many other poems by Go-Sakuramachi, it shows the personal side of a woman who passed her adult life in solitude.

Having a great talent for *waka*, the emperor left behind the *Kadō gokyō kunsho*, a *waka* treatise. Copied by Arisugawa no miya Yorihito, this work recorded more than just *waka* compositions; over the course of eight chapters, it discusses the ancient *waka* collections and poetic writings that should be carefully read, mentioning anthologies and books of poems such as the *Kokinshū*, *Shinchokusenshū*, *Ise monogatari, Genji monogatari*, Teika's *Meigetsushō*, and Juntokuin's *Yakumo mishō*, among others. *Kadō gokyō kunsho* demonstrates one aspect of the quiet, calm life of Emperor Go-Sakuramachi. For more than forty years after abdication, she poured her heart into *waka*. Go-Sakuramachi's life came to an end forty-three years after her abdication, on the second day of the eleventh intercalary month of Bunka 10 (1813). She was seventy-four years old. She is interred in the Tsuki no wa mausoleum, located in present-day Higashiyama-ku,

Kyoto.

Go-Sakuramachi's period of reign was short compared to that of the Emperor Meishō, the other Tokugawa-period female emperor. But while Meishō had a kind of guardian in the Retired Emperor Go-Mizuno'o, in Go-Sakuramachi's case, both her father, Emperor Sakuramachi, and her younger brother Emperor Monozono, only one year younger than her, had passed away. Perhaps because of that, Emperor Go-Sakuramachi showed considerable attentiveness to imperial governance. Her various concerns after retirement demonstrated the depth of her self-awareness as emperor. She was an emperor of great conviction.

Being under the control of the bakufu, the two female emperors of the Tokugawa period, Emperor Meishō and Emperor Go-Sakuramachi, did not exercise direct imperial rule. They thus appear less remarkable when compared to the female emperors of the ancient period. Meishō was an emperor backed by the bakufu, while Go-Sakuramachi was an emperor with no blood connection to the warrior shogunate. There was a 119-year gap between their rules, and they lived in periods during which social and cultural trends were ever-changing. Although the existence of these two women tends to be forgotten in the history of the Tokugawa shogunate, they should not be forgotten in the history of female emperors.

Conclusion

Across their ten reigns, the eight female emperors shared many things in common, but were also very distinctive. One recurring, common element is that of acting as intermediary emperors who were instated as placeholders to protect the family line of the imperial throne. In the *Shoku Nihongi*, Emperor Genshō is called a "middle emperor (*nakatsu tennō*)." This was most frequently the case among the female emperors. However, women were not the only rulers who fulfilled a transitional role, as this practice was often found among male emperors, as well.

There were typically three premises for the enthronement of female emperors. For Emperor Saimei and Emperor Jitō/Genmei, the imperial throne was protected by their strong personal desire to make their own child the next emperor. For Emperors Suiko, Kōgyoku, and Genshō, becoming emperor was not always a matter of will, but a necessity. And for Emperors Meishō and Go-Sakuramachi, they were enthroned not by their own wishes, but entirely on the insistence of those surrounding them. Both of these emperors were enthroned when they were still children, and the bakufu held all of the power in the political system at the time, so even when they came of age, there was never an expectation that they would act independently as emperor. In contrast, Emperor Kōken

Conclusion   *259*

was the first woman to be appointed crown prince, and, as such, she followed the same path to enthronement as a male emperor would have and was re-enthroned when Emperor Junnin was deposed. In other words, all of them ruled based on the circumstances of their individual time periods and environments, and concluding that female emperors were, by default, intermediary in nature is short-sighted.

Furthermore, as touched upon in the introduction, at some point, women who were domineering and lusted for power came to be pejoratively called "*jotei* (now translated as female emperors)," but, as we have seen here, this interpretation has no foundation in the history of these eight women. While there may have been women of such ambitions closely associated with male emperors, it is inaccurate to generalize about female emperors in such a way. Evidence of their reigns shows that many were kind, always thinking of the people, and, given the chance, took great pains to do what was best for their lands. Whatever the veracity of surviving historical records, the female emperors still accomplished their imperial duties as high-ranking individuals who took great pride in their work. Furthermore, emperors such as Genshō, Kōken, Shōtoku, Meishō, and Go-Sakuramachi fulfilled their roles while single for their entire lives, a situation not seen among adult male emperors.

It is also notable that Emperor Jitō was the first to be entrusted with government as a retired emperor to help the young Emperor Daijō, a trend that other female emperors also followed. Although Japan's *insei* (cloistered rule) system[100] is typically considered to have begun with Emperor Shirakawa at the end of the Heian period as result of the Fujiwara regency, Emperor Jitō's rule is a prior example of an administration led by retired emperors. Even then, this method of rule was not limited to the female emperors, but existed under Retired Emperor Shōmu. The two female emperors of the Tokugawa period also abdicated while young and spent many long years as retired emperors; although they did not participate in politics due to the circumstances of the time, they did provide guidance for the next generation of young emperors as a part of the court institution. If a woman becomes emperor in Japan in the future, the histories of these eighth emperors will be a critical guide to understanding Japan's imperial legacy.

[100] See footnote 4.

Contributors

Masako Hamada

Masako Hamada is an Associate Professor in the Japanese Studies Program in the Department of Global Interdisciplinary Studies as well as the Director of the Asian Studies Program at Villanova University. She has an MA in Intercultural Communication from the University of Pennsylvania and an EdD in International & Transcultural Studies from Columbia University. She is the author of various articles and books, including *Japanese Female Professors in the United States: A Comparative Study in Conflict Resolution and Intercultural Communication* (2006) and *Japanese Male Professors on American College Campuses: A Comparative Study of Conflict Management* (2012). She is a contributing editor, writer, and translator for *Phila-Nipponica: An Historic Guide to Philadelphia & Japan* (second edition, 2015).

Paula R. Curtis

Paula R. Curtis is a PhD Candidate in History at the University of Michigan specializing in medieval Japan. She received her BA in Japanese Studies from Gettysburg College (2008) and an MA in East Asian Studies from The Ohio State University (2011). She attended the Inter-University Center for Japanese Languages Studies in 2009-2010. She presently researches documentary forgery, socioeconomic networks, and commercial commoners in late medieval Japan.

Hiroko Manabe

Hiroko Manabe graduated from Kyoto University with a specialization in English Literature. She has previously taught Japanese language, culture, and translation at institutions such as the Berlitz School of Languages (Philadelphia, PA), Japan Culture Center, Jawaharlal Nehru University (New Delhi, India), Drexel University, and Villanova University.

Amy V. Heinrich

Amy Vladeck Heinrich received her PhD in Japanese Literature in 1980 from Columbia University, under the guidance of Professor Donald Keene. Following his advice, when researching her dissertation on the poetry of Saitō Mokichi, she became a member of Kiyoko Takagi's poetry group, *Uchūfū*, and attended meetings for many years. Her major publications include, as author, *Fragments of Rainbows: The Life and Poetry of Saitō Mokichi, 1882-1953* (Columbia University Press, 1983); as editor, *Currents in Japanese Culture: Translations and Transformations* (Columbia University Press, 1997); and as translator with introduction, *Memoir of the Forgetting-the-Capital Flower,* by Tanizaki Jun'ichirō (Yushodo and Columbia University Press, 2010). She retired in 2009 as Director of the C. V. Starr East Asian Library, Columbia University.

Masako Iino

Masako Iino is a Professor Emeritus and former President of Tsuda University, Tokyo. After finishing her BA at Tsuda

University (1966), she studied as a Fulbright graduate student at Syracuse University and received her MA in American history (1968). As a professor, she taught in the fields of American history, U. S. -Japan relations, and immigration studies at her alma mater for many years. She also taught at McGill University, Acadia University, and was a visiting professor at the University of California, Berkeley and Bryn Mawr College. Her numerous publications include *Another History of US-Japan Relations: Japanese Americans Swayed by the Cooperation and the Disputes between the Two Nations* (Yuhikaku, 2000). She is currently President of the Japan-U. S. Educational Exchange Promotion Foundation (Fulbright Foundation).

Richard Showstack

Richard Showstack has BAs from the University of California, Berkeley in Humanities and Psychology and an MA from San Francisco State University in Teaching English as a Foreign Language. He taught English at International Christian University in Tokyo for several years, and also co-hosted an English-language-learning show on NHK television. He is now a freelance writer/ editor/ proofreader. His published books include: *The Gift Of The Magic And Other Enchanting Character-building Stories For Smart Teenage Girls Who Want To Grow Up To Be Strong Women* (2004), and *A Horse Named Peggy And Other Enchanting Character-building Stories For Smart Teenage Boys Who Want To Grow Up To Be Good Men* (2004).

Bibliography and Further Reading

Barnes, Gina L. *State formation in Japan: Emergence of a 4th-century Ruling Elite*. London: Routledge, 2007.

Bender, Ross. "The Hachiman Cult and the Dokyo Incident." *Monumenta Nipponica* 34, no. 2 (Summer 1979): 125-153.

———. "Auspicious Omens in the Reign of the Last Empress of Nara Japan, 749-770."

Japanese Journal of Religious Studies 40, no. 1 (2013): 45-76.

———. "Changing the Calendar: Royal Political Theology and the Suppression of the

Tachibana Naramaro Conspiracy of 757." *Japanese Journal of Religious Studies* 37, no. 2 (2010): 223-245.

———. *The Edicts of the Last Empress, 749-770: A Translation from Shoku Nihongi*. CreateSpace, 2015.

———. *Nara Japan, 749-757: A Translation from Shoku Nihongi*, CreateSpace, 2015.

———. *Nara Japan, 758-763: A Translation from Shoku Nihongi*, CreateSpace, 2016.

———. *Nara Japan, 764-766: A Translation from Shoku Nihongi*, CreateSpace, 2016.

———. *Nara Japan, 767-770: A Translation from Shoku Nihongi*, CreateSpace, 2016.

Como, Michael I. *Shotoku: Ethnicity, Ritual, and Violence in the Japanese Buddhist Tradition*. Oxford and New York: Oxford University Press, 2008.

Duthie, Torquil. *Man'yōshū and the Imperial Imagination in Early Japan*. Leiden: Brill, 2014.

Kokushi daijiten henshu iinkai, *Kokushi daijiten* (14 vols), Tokyo: Yoshikawa kobunkan, 1979-1997.

Leupp, Gary P. *Male Colors: The Construction of Homosexuality in Tokugawa Japan*. Berkeley: University of California Press, 1995.

Lillehoj, Elizabeth, and John T. Carter. *Art and Palace Politics in Early Modern Japan, 1580s-1680s*. Boston: Brill, 2014.

Ooms, Herman. *Imperial Politics and Symbolics in Ancient Japan: The Tenmu Dynasty, 650-800*. Honolulu: Hawai'i Press, 2008.

Piggott, Joan R. "Chietain Pairs and Corulers: Female Sovereignty in Early Japan." In *Women and Class in Japanese History*, edited by Hitomi Tonomura, Anne Walthall, and Wakita Haruko, 17-52. Ann Arbor, MI: University of Michigan Center for Japanese Studies, 1999.

———. *The Emergence of Japanese Kingship*. Stanford: Stanford University Press, 1997.

Scheid, Bernard. "Shōmu Tennō and the Deity from Kyushu: Hachiman's Initial Rise to Prominence," *Japan Review* 27 (2014): 31-51.

von Verscheur, Charlotte. *Across the Perilous Sea: Japanese Trade with China and Korea from the Seventh to the Sixteenth Centuries*. Translated by Kristen Lee Hunter. Ithaca, NY: Cornell East Asia Series, 2006.

【本書は『八人の女帝』(2005年初版、冨山房インターナショナル発行) の英語版です】

The Eight Female Emperors of Japan
A Brief Introduction to Their Lives and Legacies

2018年9月10日　第1刷発行

著　者	高木きよ子
訳　者	浜田昌子ほか
発行者	坂 本 喜 杏
発行所	株式会社冨山房インターナショナル

〒101-0051
東京都千代田区神田神保町1-3
TEL　03(3291)2578　FAX　03(3219)4866
URL　www.fuzambo-intl.com

印　刷	株式会社冨山房インターナショナル
製　本	加藤製本株式会社

©Kiyoko Takagi 2018 Printed in Japan

落丁本・乱丁本はお取り替えいたします。
ISBN 978-4-86600-052-7

梅風

柳

春月